SCRABBLE
BRAND Crossword Game

PLAY TO WIN

HarperCollins Publishers
Westerhill Road
Bishopbriggs
Glasgow
G64 2QT

First edition 2009

Reprint 10 9 8 7 6 5 4 3 2 1 0

ISBN 978-0-00-732418-7

© HarperCollins Publishers 2009

Scrabble ® is a registered
trademark of J. W. Spear & Sons Ltd,
a subsidiary of Mattel, Inc. © 2009
Mattel, Inc.

Collins ® is a registered trademark
of HarperCollins Publishers Limited

www.collinslanguage.com

A catalogue record for this book is
available from the British Library

Typeset by Davidson Pre-Press,
Glasgow

Printed in Italy by
LEGO Spa, Lavis (Trento)

Contents

1 Introducing Scrabble   1

2 The rules of the game   8

3 Two- and three-letter words   20

4 Dealing with **J**, **Q**, **X** and **Z**   34

5 Using the **S**   45

6 Using the blank   53

7 Finding the bonus words   58

8 Some seven-letter lists   81

9 Some eight-letter lists   99

10 Help with unusual letter combinations   117

11 Ending the game   137

12 Other forms of Scrabble   147

13 Taking it further   152

Allowable word forms   163

Glossary of terms   166

Quick reference lists

   Alphabetical list of two-letter words   171

   Alphabetical list of useful three-letter words

      appearing in this book   172

   Alphabetical list of useful **J**, **Q**, **X** and **Z** words   173

Answers to puzzles   174

Useful links   185

1 Introducing Scrabble

Games are strange things. Some, like chess and backgammon, look terribly complicated to an onlooker who doesn't know the rules. It seems that you must have to be some sort of expert to play these games. Scrabble is different somehow.

Even if someone had never seen the game in their life before, it probably wouldn't take them long to pick up the general idea if they watched a game being played. The scoring might take them a little longer but, fundamentally, it's easy enough – just place the letters on the board to form words, like in a crossword. This makes most people think that once they've grasped that, they know all they need to know – perhaps all there is to know – about the game.

This is very far from the truth. Scrabble, like chess, backgammon or bridge, has a high skill factor. And that doesn't just mean knowing lots of words. A strong player will certainly know a lot of words that the average person, even the average reasonably well-educated person, will never have heard of. But you have to know the right words. A professor of English will find it no help at all in Scrabble to know words like **CATACHRESTICAL** or **SOMNILOQUENCE**. You can beat the Prof. if you know words like **OURIE** and **ZAX**.

> *Scrabble facts – In 1985, two Royal Marines on a training exercise on Brabant Island, Antarctica, fell down a crevasse; luckily, one of them had a Scrabble set in his kit-bag and they passed the five days that they waited to be rescued playing Scrabble.*

Increasing your enjoyment

A game of Scrabble is basically a series of problems. How many times have you yelled in frustration at picking too many vowels or consonants, or cursed the fates for giving you an unwanted **J**, **Q**, **X** or **Z**? How often have you looked at the tiles on your rack and thought, 'I bet these make a seven-letter word', but not been able to work out what it was? How much more fun would the game be if you knew how to deal with these situations?

> *Scrabble facts* – *In a two-person game, most people playing with family and friends will average between 180 and 300 points per game. Stronger players can average more than 400 points.*

Making the most of 'good' tiles on your rack and limiting the damage from 'bad' ones is what makes your game more enjoyable, and improves your chances of winning. And that's what this book is all about.

> *Scrabble facts* – *The highest-ever score for a single word was 392 for* **CAZIQUES**, *played by Karl Khoshnaw of Richmond, Surrey, in 1982. The highest score for a game is a massive 1049 by Phil Appleby of Lymington, Hampshire.*

It won't happen automatically. It'll take a bit of concentration, a bit of practice, a bit of memory work. But if you enjoy Scrabble already, reading this book and taking on board what it suggests will bring you a lot more success at the game, and – more importantly – a lot more pleasure.

Who invented Scrabble?

Alfred Butts was an architect, but in the 1930s he was unemployed as a result of the Great Depression. He was also a word-game enthusiast, doing crosswords and tinkering with anagrams.

First there was Lexiko

Hoping to make some money, he developed a game called Lexiko. This involved players drawing seven tiles, then simply taking turns to discard tiles and draw new ones until they could make a seven-letter word. The first player to do so won. There was no board, no points and no element of interlocking your word with what had already been played. No games manufacturer was interested in producing it, partly because in the Depression most people presumably had little money to spend on games, but partly, one suspects, because it sounds a bit boring.

> **Scrabble facts** – Early names for Scrabble included **Lexiko**, **Criss-Crosswords** and **It**.

Butts then introduced point values for the different letters. When a player had won a round by playing a seven-letter word, the others could play whatever words they could make from their hand, and lose the point values of the remaining tiles.

Determined as ever, Alfred tried again to have the game produced commercially, but still with no success. As an architect, Butts would have known that everything takes time, whether building a house or perfecting a game. He kept refining his invention, and eventually added the board, the premium squares and the crossword-style building up of words that we know from the game today.

Scrabble is born

By now, you might think that the manufacturers would have been falling over themselves to produce the game, but still Butts had no success. In 1939 he met James Brunot, a civil servant with an entrepreneurial streak. Brunot was immediately intrigued by the game. He played around with the idea, refined it a bit more and, like Butts, tried to get it onto the market. But it was now the early 1940s, and the world had more pressing matters to attend to. Finally, in 1949, Brunot formed his own business, the Production and Marketing Company, and the game – by now, after a few more name changes, called Scrabble – was finally ready to go into the shops.

> **Scrabble facts** – *Butts based the frequency of letters in the Scrabble set on how often each occurred in headlines in the* New York Times, *the* Herald Tribune *and the* Evening Post.

Unfortunately, even after 18 years or so of development, Scrabble was still no overnight success. Sales were slow, and Brunot was losing money. In the first three years, no more than 20,000 sets were sold. Things were looking grim for Alfred and James, and Scrabble might well have faded away there and then. Then Jack Strauss went on holiday.

Holiday success

Strauss was a shopkeeper, and he discovered Scrabble while on a summer break with some friends. He loved the game and, on his return to work, promptly placed an order and organized a major promotion for the game in the store. This might not have mattered much if Jack Strauss had just been any shopkeeper. In fact, he was the chairman of Macy's, one of the largest department stores in New York. With that kind of power to push it, Scrabble was well and truly on its way. Sales in the low thousands were transformed into millions, and Brunot's and Butts' long struggle was over.

Scrabble facts – There are daily or weekly puzzles or columns based on Scrabble in The Times, Daily Telegraph, Daily Mail *and* Daily Express.

Because its Orthodox readers cannot write on a Saturday, the Jewish Chronicle *has a weekly crossword designed to be done by placing tiles on a Scrabble board.*

Scrabble around the world

Scrabble soon spread through the English-speaking world, and it wasn't long until the game was being produced in foreign languages too.
Of course, this required a re-evaluation of the point values and frequency of each tile for every new language.

*   If you struggle without an **E**, spare a thought for the Dutch, who are such **E** addicts that they have a whopping 18 of them in a set, but only 20 other vowels in total.

*   A Russian set has 33 different letters plus two blanks. Not surprisingly all these letters cannot fit into 98 tiles, so Russian Scrabble has a mighty 126 tiles per set, including the blanks.

Scrabble facts – Amongst the languages you can play Scrabble in are:
Afrikaans, Arabic, Danish, Dutch, Finnish, Portuguese, Russian, Yiddish

Scrabble is now played by millions of people across the world, and it regularly tops the chart of best-selling games. About 100 million sets have been sold worldwide since it all started in 1948! Walk into any house in Britain, and there's a 50 per cent chance that it will have a Scrabble set lurking somewhere. The game is said to be popular in homes ranging from Buckingham Palace to prisons.

> **Scrabble facts** – *Kylie Minogue is a big fan.*
>
> *Snooker players use it to relax in the long intervals between matches – Steve Davis and James Wattana are reported to be particularly hot, clearly masters of the Q as well as the cue.*

Parents can introduce young children to the game with **My First Scrabble**, and then they can move on to **Junior Scrabble** when they are a little older. There is also a Braille version of the game, with raised dots on the tiles and the premium squares.

And nowadays, of course, no range is complete without the computer version. You can buy a CD-ROM to play against your computer, choosing an appropriate skill level so that you always (luck permitting) get a good, close game. But be warned, the computer version of the game is addictive. You can find out about other forms of Scrabble in Chapter 12.

> **Scrabble facts** – *To celebrate the game's 50th anniversary in 1998, two teams from the Army and the Navy played a game on the pitch at Wembley Stadium. The side of each tile was 1.25 metres (4 feet) and the side of the board was over 18.5 metres (60 feet)!*

Alfred Butts died in 1993, so he lived long enough to see the worldwide success the game had become. Millions of sets, addicts by the tens of thousands, even Scrabble clubs and World Championships – could he have dreamt of what he was starting when he came up with his curious little game, back in those dark, depressed days of 1931?

2 The rules of the game

Every Scrabble set contains a copy of the rules, but just in case you've lost yours, or you haven't actually got yourself a Scrabble set yet, this chapter gives you a quick guide.

Setting up the game

1   Open out the board and give each player one of the tile racks.
    The bag containing the tiles should be placed to one side of the board, within easy reach of all the players.

2   One player acts as score-keeper for all the players, and will need a pen and paper. (Alternatively, all players can keep score as a check.) See Rules 7 to 11 for more details about scoring.

3   Each player draws one tile from the bag. The nearest to the beginning of the alphabet starts. In the event of a tie, the tied players draw again. A blank beats an **A**. The letters are then put back in the bag and the bag is shaken.

4   The player who starts picks seven tiles from the bag, and places them on his or her rack without letting the other players see them. Passing to the left, the other players in turn also pick seven tiles and place them on their rack.

The first move

5   The first player makes a word from two to seven of his or her letters and places that word on the board, either across (from left to right) or down (from top to bottom). One letter must go on the centre square (in most sets this is marked with a star or similar marker). The player counts his or her score (the first word counts as a double word score, see scoring, below) and announces it. He or she then takes as many tiles from the bag as have just been played, thus giving seven tiles on the rack again.

Second and subsequent moves

6   Play passes to the left. Each player makes his or her move by adding from one to seven of their own tiles to those already on the board. The letters played, either across or down, must themselves form a valid word, and they must interlock with the letters already on the board, crossword-style, so that all additional words formed are also valid words. Again, the move is completed by the counting and announcing of the score, and the replenishment of the rack back to seven tiles by picking from the bag.

Scoring

7   The basic score for each tile is shown by a small number, from one to ten, printed in the bottom right-hand corner of the tile. The list below shows the score for each letter.

Letter	No. in set	Score	Letter	No. in set	Score
A	9	1	L	4	1
E	12	1	M	2	3
I	9	1	N	6	1
O	8	1	P	2	3
U	4	1	Q	1	10
			R	6	1
B	2	3	S	4	1
C	2	3	T	6	1
D	4	2	V	2	4
F	2	4	W	2	4
G	3	2	X	1	8
H	2	4	Y	2	4
J	1	8	Z	1	10
K	1	5	BLANK	2	0

8   The board contains a number of special scoring squares.

- A letter placed on a **_Double Letter_** square has its value doubled.
- A letter placed on a **_Triple Letter_** square has its value tripled.
- If any letter of a word has been placed on a **_Double Word_** square the complete word has its entire score doubled.
- If any letter of a word has been placed on a **_Triple Word_** square then the word has its entire score tripled.

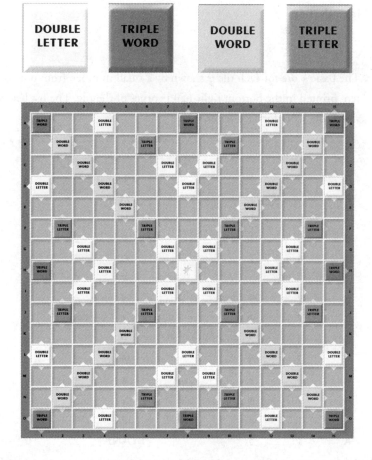

9   When two or more words are formed in one move, each is scored. The common letter is counted (with full premium values, if any) in the score for each word.

MOTIF =
$(3 + 1 + 1 + 1 + (4 \times 2)) \times 2$
$= 28$
F is on a Double Letter square. **M** is on a Double Word square. The total letter score is added up first and then multiplied by 2 because of the Double Word square.
FIRM $= 4 + 1 + 1 + 3 = 9$
Only the tile value of **F** is used. The Double Letter square only benefits the player who placed **F** on the board.

FIRMS =
$(4 + 1 + 1 + 3 + 1) \times 2$
$= 20$
WRITS =
$((4 \times 2) + 1 + 1 + 1 + 1)$
$\times 2 = 24$
Total score = 44
The **S** is on a Double Word square so both **FIRMS** and **WRITS** score double. **W** is on a Double Letter square.

10 Premium squares are only counted in the move in which they are covered. If the word is modified in a subsequent move, tiles on premium squares count at face value only.

11 Any player playing all seven of his or her tiles in one move scores a **bonus** of 50 points in addition to the regular score for the move.

Miscellaneous

12 There are two blank tiles in the set, which may be used as any letter. When a blank is played, the player must nominate which letter the blank represents. The blank then remains as that letter for the rest of the game. A blank tile has a score of zero, but if a blank is placed on a Double Word or Triple Word square, the word is still doubled or tripled, as appropriate.

Scrabble tip – Another rule some people like to incorporate is to allow the blank to be lifted from the board and replaced with the letter it represents, allowing the player to re-use the blank. While not part of the official rules, this is a useful way to keep the game moving, and I would not discourage it, particularly for beginners.

13 Rather than playing any tiles on the board, a player may instead choose to change any or all of his or her tiles. To do this, the player places the tiles to be changed to one side, picks the same number of new tiles from the bag, and then puts the old tiles back in the bag. A change counts as a score of zero, and a player cannot change and make a scoring move in the same turn.

14 Any other player may challenge a player's move, if he or she considers that any of the words made are not valid words. A challenge must be

made before the player has picked and looked at any of the replacement tiles. The word should then be checked in a dictionary or an official Scrabble word source. If the word is wrong, the player must take back his or her tiles from that move, and gets a score of zero.

> ***Scrabble tip*** – *Some 'house rules' allow players to consult a dictionary before playing their move, but most keen players do not favour this. It can be useful to have a dictionary around if a player challenges a word after it has been played. It's a good idea to have a dictionary that gives plurals and different verb forms (see page 163).*

Ending the game

15 When there are no tiles left in the bag, play continues until one player has used all the tiles on his or her rack. Every other player then has the total value of their unplayed tiles deducted from their score, and the player who has played all his or her tiles has the total value of all unplayed tiles added to his or her score. If no player can play off all their tiles, each player has the value of their unplayed tiles deducted from their score.

Some example moves

To help get you under way, follow through the moves shown on these boards.

Move 1
GATE scores 5, doubled, scores 10 points.

Move 2
PITCH, with the **I** and **C** doubled, scores 16 points.

Move 3
GLARED, with the **G** and **E** tripled, score 14, plus 6 for **AGATE**, scores 20 points.

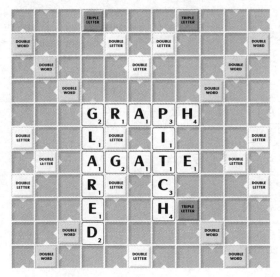

Move 4
GRAPH, with the **H** tripled, scores 19 points.

Move 5
BIOGRAPHER scores 18 points. (Note the **H** is not re-tripled.)

Move 6
OMIT scores 6 and **ID** scores 3, both doubled, making 18. **ME** scores 4 and **OR** 2, for a total score of 24 points.

Move 7

TENSILE, covering two double word squares, is doubled then redoubled, scoring 7 × 4 = 28, plus 7 for **AGATES**, scores 35 points.

Move 8

The **T** of **HONESTY** is doubled, then the whole word is doubled, scoring 20 (with the **H** as a blank scoring zero). Add 19 for **BIOGRAPHERS**, plus the 50-point bonus for using all seven tiles, for a total score of 89 points.

You may not spot words like **BIOGRAPHER, HONESTY** and **TENSILE** right away, but these moves have been shown to demonstrate the variety of ways you can 'build' a move within the basic rules, and how to score them.

Knowing if a word is allowed

It's very annoying when you play a word, only to have it disallowed by those you are playing with. Use *Collins Scrabble Lists* to adjudicate on any challenges. This lists every allowable word in strict alphabetical order, except that very long words, those with ten letters or more, are confined to a separate section at the end. No arguing about the plural of octopus or whether you can have **SUBLIMER** or **HONESTEST**.

If you haven't got *Collins Scrabble Lists*, you and your fellow-players will have to do a bit of adjudicating from time to time. Dictionaries will generally list only a base word, such as **TABLE** and will not specifically show **TABLES, TABLED, TABLING** or **TABLINGS**. Before starting play it's worth agreeing a few guidelines as to what you're going to allow and what you aren't. If you want to find out more, look at the section at the back of the book on allowable word forms.

> *Scrabble tip – By using the most recent edition of* Collins Scrabble Lists *the allowable word list stays up to date; new words are being coined or accepted into English all the time, and you don't want to be prevented from playing* **EMAIL, EURO, CHAV, ZIT, BIRYANI** *or any of a host of others.*

Using a large word source is the only way to bring into play the wealth of fascinating words which we will be looking at throughout this book, and which your own dictionary may not have. Some people feel that the more words are allowed in the game, the more it becomes just a memory exercise. Learning the words is certainly important, but having a large number of words at your disposal allows you to display a fuller range of Scrabble skills than would otherwise be the case.

> **Scrabble facts** – *It's difficult to assess how many words the average English speaker knows or uses, but estimates range from 40,000 to 75,000. Yet there are a whopping 267,633 words eligible for Scrabble in English!*
> *Lots to learn then...*

3 Two- and three-letter words

Now that we've got the rules sorted out, it's time to take a look at how you can improve your game. A major part of that consists of having a large armoury of useful words at your disposal. You may think the longer the word you know is, the more useful it will be, as it's likely to score more. However, in fact, the key to a good Scrabble vocabulary is a good knowledge of short words, particularly words of two and three letters.

Low scoring play
Adding the letters **F, A, R, E** to **TEAM** to give **AFTER**
gives you a score of 7.

Short words are, of course, invaluable for helping you complete a game and to use difficult letters. They have another great use, which can really help you boost your score. You can use short words to join or 'hook' the word you want to play on to the board, by playing parallel to another word. You will usually make more than one word each turn and so make a higher score than just by crossing over another word. Look at the two different ways of playing on the two boards shown here.

Notice that the high scoring play has scored 18 more points than the low scoring play. This score was only possible because of the word **FA** (think musical scales).

High scoring play
Adding the letters **F**, **A**, **R**, **E** to **TEAM** to gives a score of 25.

Two-letter words

Here is the first, essential thing you have to know to improve your game: **know all the allowable two-letter words.** There are 124 of them in *Collins Official Scrabble Dictionary*, but to make the list more manageable, you can divide them into three groups:

- The ones you already know.
- The ones you already know, but may not have realized were words.
- The ones you probably don't know.

Commonly known two-letter words

Here are the words you most likely know and which will appear in most dictionaries:

AH	AM	AN	AS	AT	AX	AY
BE	BY					
DO						
EH						
GO						
HA	HE	HI	HO			
ID	IF	IN	IS	IT		
LA	LO					
MA	ME	MY				
NO						
OF	OH	ON	OR	OX		
PA						
SO						
TO						
UP	US					
WE						
YE						

Less well-known two-letter words

There are then a good selection of words that you probably know but were unsure whether they were allowable Scrabble words. As we enter less familiar areas, it is useful to know the meaning of the special words you use, not least so you can convince those you are playing with that the words are for real.

Contracted words

AD	advertisement
BI	bisexual
MO	moment
OP	operation
PO	chamberpot
RE	regarding
TA	thank you

Exclamations and interjections

AW	variant of **ALL**
ER	sound made when hesitating in conversation
HM	sound made to express hesitation or doubt
MM	expression of enjoyment of taste or smell
OI, OY	shout to attract attention
OW	exclamation of pain
OY	shout to attract attention (*or* grandchild)
SH	exclamation to request silence or quiet (*or used instead of* **SHILLING**)
ST	used to attract attention
UH, UM, UR	used to express hesitation or uncertainty in speech
YA	*variant of* **YOU**
YO	used as a greeting or to attract someone's attention

Then there are letters of the alphabet when spelt out. At the end of the list are some names for some Greek letters.

Letters of the alphabet

AR	letter **R**
EF	letter **F**
EL	letter **L** *or* an abbreviated version of **ELEVATED RAILWAY**, as in Chicago
EM	letter **M** *or* a standard unit of measurement in typography
EN	letter **N** *or* a unit of measurement that is half an em
ES	letter **S**
EX	letter **X** *or* a preposition meaning not including or an informal name for a former husband or wife
PE	letter **P**
TE	letter **T**

MU, **NU**, **PI** and **XI** are all Greek letters

Unfamiliar two-letter words

The third group of words will be less familiar, but, as a result, likely to be very useful once you have remembered them. They are listed below, and then some explanations follow.

AA	AB	AE	AG	AI	AL
BA	BO				
CH					
DA	DE	DI			
EA	ED	EE	ET		
FA	FE	FY			
GI	GU				
IO					
JA	JO				
KA	KI	KO	KY		
LI					
MI					
NA	NE	NY			
OB	OD	OE	OM	OO	OS	OU
QI					
SI					
TI					
UG	UN	UT			
WO					
XU					
YU					
ZA	ZO				

If all this looks a bit gobbledygookish, you may be surprised to know that even some of these are more familiar to you than you might realise:

- An **AB** is an abdominal muscle, as in toning up your abs and your pecs.
- **OM** is what Buddhists chant as part of their prayers.
- **AA** is a word from Hawaiian, meaning a rough volcanic rock. Its opposite, smooth volcanic rock, is called **PAHOEHOE**.
- **ZO** is a Himalayan cross-breed of a yak and a cow, also spelt **ZHO**, **DZO**, **DZHO** or **DSO**, useful Scrabble words every man-jack of them.

Just to help you along, here are a list of meanings for the rest of them.

AE	one
AG	agriculture
AI	shaggy-coated slow-moving South American animal
AL	Asian shrub or tree
BA	Ancient Egyptian symbol for the soul
BO	exclamation used to startle or surprise someone
CH	archaic form of **EKE** (to lengthen or stretch)
DA	Burmese knife
DE	of, from
DI	plural of **DEUS** (god)
EA	river
ED	editor
EE	eye (*Scots*)
ET	ate (*dialect*)
FA	fourth degree of any major scale (*music*)
FE	fee
FY	exclamation of disapproval
GI	loose-fitting white suit worn in judo and karate

GU	type of violin used in Shetland
IO	type of moth
JA	yes (*in South Africa*)
JO	sweetheart (*Scots*)
KA	spirit dwelling as a vital force in man or a statue
KI	Japanese martial art
KO	traditional digging tool (*in New Zealand*)
KY	cows (*Scots*)
LI	Chinese measurement of distance
MI	third degree of any major scale (*music*)
NA	no (*Scots*)
NE	nor
NY	near
OB	expression of opposition
OD	hypothetical force formerly thought to be responsible for many natural phenomena
OE	grandchild
OO	wool (*Scots*)
OS	mouthlike opening
OU	man, chap
QI	vital life force (*in Oriental medicine and martial arts*)
SI	seventh degree of any major scale (*music*)
TI	seventh degree of any major scale (*music*)
UG	to hate
UN	one
UT	the note C
WO	woe
XU	Vietnamese currency unit
YU	jade
ZA	pizza

Have a look back at the two-letter words every so often as you're going through the book. Once you're happy with the first two groups (i.e. the common ones, the contractions, the interjections and the letters), have a real go at mastering the unusual ones. They really are the essential first step to improving your game.

Three-letter words

But it doesn't end there. *Three-letter words are almost as important as the twos* for helping you build up your moves – and there are a lot more of them. Unless you have a lot of time and aptitude to study lists, or have a photographic memory, it will take you a few months to get to grips fully with the threes. Take them gradually, starting with the ones containing **J**, **Q**, **X** and **Z**. You won't need to know all of them before your game starts to improve.

Here are some of the most useful threes:

Containing **J**

GJU type of violin used in Shetland

JAP to splash

JEE mild exclamation of surprise

JIZ wig

JOE sweetheart (*Scots*)

RAJ British government in India before 1947

TAJ tall conical cap worn as a mark of distinction by Muslims

Containing **Q**

QAT evergreen shrubs

QIS plural of **QI** (*vital life force*)

QUA in the capacity of

SUQ open-air market place, e.g. in North Africa

Containing X

DEX dextroamphetamine

GOX gaseous oxygen

HOX to hamstring

KEX any of several large hollow-stemmed umbelliferous plants, such as chervil

RAX to stretch or extend

REX king

VOX voice

WEX wax

WOX wax

XIS plural of **XI** (*14th letter in the Greek alphabet*)

ZAX axe

Containing Z

You can remember some of the **Z**-threes in sets of two and three:

BEZ	part of a deer's horn	**BIZ**	business
CAZ	casual	**COZ, CUZ**	cousin
FEZ	tasselled cap	**FIZ**	fizz
MIZ	misery	**MOZ**	hex
SAZ	Middle Eastern stringed instrument	**SEZ**	informal spelling of 'says'
		ZIG, ZAG	to change direction sharply

Other useful Z-threes

ADZ tool with cutting blade at right angles to the handle

DZO animal that is a cross between a cow and a yak

JIZ wig

ZAX axe

ZEP type of long sandwich

ZOA independent animal bodies (*plural of* **ZOON**)

ZOS plural of **ZO** (*animal that is a cross between a cow and a yak*)

These lists are not exhaustive, but they will get you started. You won't always be able to fit in a **QUIVER**, a **ZEBRA** or an **ANNEX**, so you need to know a good selection of these shorter words to help you play your high-scoring letters – preferably for a more than face-value score.

Threes containing awkward letters

Other useful three-letter words are those that can help you get rid of awkward letters like **U** and **V**, or which allow you to use excess vowels. You should try to remember:

AIA	female servant, usually Indian or Malay
AUA	yellow-eye mullet (*Maori*)
AUE	Maori exclamation of pain or astonishment
AYU	small Japanese fish
EAU	river
UVA	grape
VAU, VAV	sixth letter of the Hebrew alphabet

Threes as 'hooks'

By 'hooks', we mean words which can be formed by adding one letter at the beginning or end of another word. Threes which are hooks of frequently used twos can be very helpful. You'll find that you play **ZO** fairly often now that you know it, which is why it's especially good to know **AZO**, **DZO** and **ZOA** – so that you can add the extra letter to an already-played **ZO**, making another word at right angles while you're doing it.

If you look back at the example moves shown in the previous chapter, notice that we didn't just add an **A** to **GATE** to make **AGATE** – we made a whole new word, **GLARED**, as well. This is why these hook-words of any length are so useful. The lists of useful **J**, **Q**, **X** and **Z** words above have been compiled partly with hooks in mind. Here are a few more commonly played twos with the threes you can make from them:

AA:	**AAH**	**AAL**	**AAS**	**BAA**	**CAA**	**FAA**	**MAA**
CH:	**ACH**	**CHA**	**CHE**	**CHI**	**ECH**	**ICH**	**OCH**
HM:	**HMM**	**OHM**					
KY:	**KYE**	**KYU**	**SKY**				

By now, you're no doubt wondering what these odd-looking words mean. As with the twos, some are more familiar than you might realize – **BAA** and **MAA** are the cries of a sheep and a goat respectively, **CHA** is tea, **ACH** and **OCH** are what you say in Scotland when you're annoyed, **HMM** is what you say if you're puzzled, and **AAS** is the plural of the rough volcanic rock **AA**. Here are some more meanings:

AAH	to exclaim in surprise
AAL	Asian shrub or tree
CAA	to call (*Scots*)
FAA	to fall (*Scots*)
CHE	dialect form of I
CHI	22nd letter of the Greek alphabet
ECH, ICH	to eke out
KYE	Korean fundraising meeting
KYU	in judo, one of the five grades for inexperienced competitors
OHM	unit of electrical resistance

> *Scrabble facts – The only letter which does not feature in any two-letter word is **V**. There are no twos ending in **C**, **J**, **K**, **Q** or **Z**.*

Don't worry about meanings

A word of advice – don't get too hung-up on meanings. It's a familiar, plaintive cry when someone new to a Scrabble club has an unfamiliar word played against them: 'What does that mean?'. It only adds to their bafflement when, as often as not, the answer comes back, 'I don't know'. It comes back to what has been said before – it's not knowing lots of words that wins you games, it's knowing the right words.

Experienced players build up a stockpile of words that they know will prove useful to them again and again. Sometimes the words have interesting meanings which can help you remember them. But often it's just another fish or plant, or a word Shakespeare used, and which has lain, dusty and unloved, at the back of the cupboard of English words ever since. Until, that is, Scrabble players came along, blew the dust off and started using it. Some of the meanings worth knowing are given in this book, but there is no rule that says you have to know the meaning of every word you play and, at the risk of incurring the wrath of the purists, I would suggest that it's very often all right just to know the word because it's good for Scrabble and not to worry about the meaning.

Another reason it is not *de rigueur* to ask about meanings during a game is that you might seem to be fishing for useful information, such as whether the word is a noun, verb or adjective, and therefore whether you can put an **S** or some other letter after it. The time to ask about meanings is after a game, not during it.

> *Scrabble tip – You can get rid of excess **I**s and **U**s with **IWI** (a Maori tribe), **ULU** (type of knife) and **UTU** (a reward). You can then use hooks to turn them into **KIWI**, **ZULU** and **TUTU**.*

When you are ready, you can find complete lists of three-letter words on the internet. In the meantime, you will be doing fine if you learn the twos and make a start on the threes highlighted in this chapter. You'll soon wonder how you ever managed to play without **AIA**, **AUA**, **WEX** or **WOX**.

HAVE A GO
CHALLENGE NO. 1

First, work out the seven-letter word you have on your rack.
It shouldn't be too difficult – think of colours or fruit.
Then can you find two places to play it on the board shown?
Remember those two- and three-letter words.

Your rack is **A E G N O R S**

4 Dealing with J, Q, X and Z

Many players don't like to pick 'the big tiles' – **J**, **Q**, **X** and **Z**. They think that because there are fewer words in which to play them, they'll be hard to get rid of, and perhaps will even end up on their rack at the end of the game, costing them a handful of points. This is wrong. The big tiles are, *usually*, good tiles to pick.

The big tiles
You have already seen the two-letter words and some of the threes containing **J**, **Q**, **X** and **Z**. Right away you have an armoury of words that will help you play these tiles.

Get points with short words
The good thing about these small words is that they may well help you play a big tile for a worthwhile score. Remind yourself of the twos containing 'the big four':

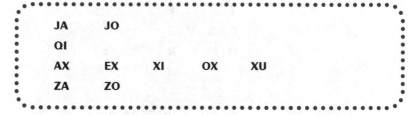

JA	JO			
QI				
AX	EX	XI	OX	XU
ZA	ZO			

Have a look at this section of a board in play:

Your rack:
D E I K L Q U

You could play **QUITE** using the **T** on the board, scoring 16. But with your new-found knowledge of **QI**, you can play **QI** both ways, slotting in another two-letter word, **ID**, as well for a very healthy 65 points:

Playing **QI** scores 65 points.

In a similar way, how would you score more than 60 points with this board and rack?

Your rack:
A D F I J O P

You should see right away that the Triple Letter square is the one which is going to pay the dividend. Playing the **J** alone to make **JO** scores 25. But can you play a word downwards as well to get the **J** tripled again? **JO** doesn't fit in this case because you can't have **OTE**, but there's no problem with **ATE**. So play **JA** downwards, also making **JO** and **ATE**, and you're getting somewhere – 53 points for doing very little. Even better, add the **P** to the end of **JA** making **JAP**, turning **LATE** into **PLATE**, and you've bagged yourself another 10 – 63 for the move which is shown on the next page.

Playing **JAP** scores 63.

Always be on the lookout for these small but profitable moves when you have one of the big tiles. The **X**, which forms two-letter words with all the vowels (**AX EX XI OX XU**), is particularly useful for this tactic.

> *Scrabble tip – Always try to play the **J**, **Q**, **X** and **Z** tiles on premium squares for extra points.*

Get points with longer words

Another great way to get big scores with the big tiles is to look for 'double-letter–double-word' slots, or, even better, 'triple-letter–double-word' or 'double-letter–triple-word'. It works like this. Remember that if one of the letters in your word covers a Premium *Letter* square, and another covers a Premium *Word* square, the appropriate letter is doubled or tripled before the whole word. So it's another way of making a letter count for a mighty *six times* its face value. You need to make sure that it's a high-scoring tile that gets the six-times treatment.

With a rack of **E E I N O S** plus a **J**, **Q**, or **Z**, there are opportunities for multiple scores.

Look at the situation on the board shown above. On your rack you have **E E I N O S** plus one of the big tiles. Can you see where you could get your big tile doubled then redoubled, or doubled then tripled, or tripled then doubled, if it was a **J**, a **Q** or a **Z**?

Of course, you need to think here of rather longer words than the two- and three-letter ones we have been using up to now. There are plenty of common five- and six-letter words, even with the big tiles in them, and none of the words you are looking for here is unusual. The boards opposite show you some possible solutions.

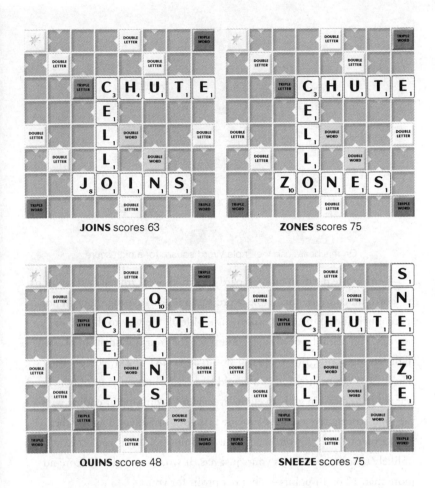

JOINS scores 63

ZONES scores 75

QUINS scores 48

SNEEZE scores 75

Score with **J**, **Q**, **X** or **Z** on the Triple Word square

If no opportunities like the ones shown above present themselves when you have a big tile, you can often get a good score simply by mopping up a handy Triple Word square.

On this board use the Triple Word square for a high-score.

Look at the position on the board shown above. Ordinarily it wouldn't be worth much to use this Triple Word square. Low-scoring tiles will not score much and, if the left-hand row is usable all the way to the top or bottom, you could be opening a good place for your opponent to play a high-scoring bonus. But if you can slot in **JET**, **QAT** or **ZIT**, you pocket a handy 30 or 36 points, and you would be very unlucky if your opponent was ready to move in with an eight-letter word beginning or ending with the high-scoring tile you have provided. If your opponent does use the high-scorer to make a word that isn't a 50-point bonus, it would be most unlikely to score as many as yours just has. It would quite likely score no more than 12 or 14 points – a big net profit for you.

Useful four- and five-letter words with J, Q, X and Z

JUGA   plural of **JUGUM**, a small process at the base of each forewing in certain insects

JORAM   large drinking bowl

JORUM   large drinking bowl

AFLAJ	plural of **FALAJ**
FALAJ	water channel
AQUA	water
QUATE	fortune
QUINE	a young, unmarried woman or girl (*Scots*)
TRANQ	tranquiliser
IXIA	southern African plant of the iris family
PREX	US college president
SOREX	a shrew or related animal
XENIA	influence of pollen upon the form of the fruit that develops after pollination
ZEIN	protein occurring in maize
ZILA	administrative district in India
ZAIRE	currency used in the former Zaire

But the big tiles aren't always good

There are times when you don't want to pull one of these high-scorers out of the bag: when you're close to a bonus, and, sometimes, when you're close to the end of a game.

Breaking up a bonus word

If you have six low-scoring tiles, well balanced between vowels and consonants, and with not too many duplicates, you should be well on your way to making a seven-letter bonus word. Picking **J**, **Q**, **X** or **Z** at that stage just screws the whole thing up, unless you're lucky enough to pick, say, a **Z** to a rack of **A E I N S T**, which you can then arrange into **ZANIEST**. Usually you just have to play the high-scorer as quickly as possible for a low score, such as using the **Z** to make **ZO** for 11 points.

Pulling out a **Q** in such circumstances can be a real challenge. You need to know that there are some words that use a **Q** without a **U**, many of Arabic origin. Here are some examples of allowed words:

QI	vital life force (*in Oriental medicine and martial arts*)
QAT	white-flowered evergreen shrub whose leaves have narcotic properties
QADI	judge in a Muslim country
QAID	chief
QOPH	19th letter of the Hebrew alphabet
WAQF	religious or charitable endowment in Muslim law
FAQIR	Muslim who spurns worldly possessions
QANAT	underground irrigation channel
QIBLA	direction of Mecca, to which Muslims turn in prayer
TALAQ	Muslim form of divorce

Sometimes you are faced with the dilemma of whether to break up your promising combination (**A E I N S T** or whatever) for the sake of getting around 20 points for your high scorer rather than about 11 or so. How much easier if you had drawn an **R** for **RETAINS** or **G** for **SEATING**.

At the end of a game

The other time you may not want to see a big tile arriving on your rack is towards the end of the game. It depends on whether there is somewhere to play it for at least 20 points or so. If there is, it can win you a close game. If not, you either have to play it off for what you can (possibly giving your opponent a chance to play out and leave you with the rest of your letters on your rack), or conversely, get rid of the rest of your letters for whatever you can and perhaps be stuck with the biggie. In some cases, if the board is blocked, you might not be able to get rid of it at all.

HAVE A GO
CHALLENGE NO. 2

In the board shown, can you find a move that scores 45?
And can you find a move that scores over 55?

Your rack is **D E I J N O S**

HAVE A GO
CHALLENGE NO. 3

Using the board shown, can you score over 50 by playing six tiles?
In another part of the board, can you score over 60 by playing six tiles?
Can you achieve a higher score by playing fewer tiles?

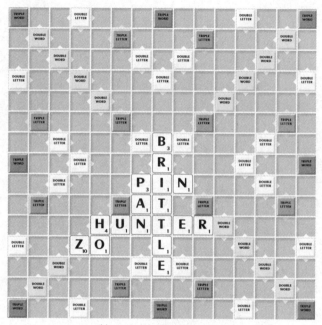

Your rack is **A E L M Q S U**

5 Using the S

Although **S** is only worth one point, it's much more valuable than you might think, because it can help you form seven-letter words and score 50 bonus points.

If you look at a game played between two good club players, and one between two less experienced players, a few differences will quickly be obvious.

- The stronger players will have played plenty of those unusual two- and three-letter words we have already looked at.
- There will be more parallel plays, resulting in solid blocks of tiles, rather than words which criss-cross through each other.
- There will be more seven- and eight-letter words played for 50-point bonuses.

This chapter will focus on the third of these, and in particular, how to use four of the six best tiles in the set – the four **S**s. The other two tiles, the two blanks, will be covered in the next chapter.

Why is the S so useful?

Look around you and come up with the first few words that come into your head. You might think of **CHAIR**, **TABLE**, **BOOK**, **SIT** and **READ**. Depending on who's in the room with you, you could come up with **MAN**, **WOMAN**, **HUSBAND**, **WIFE**, **BOY**, **GIRL**.

And what does every one of those words have in common? Yes, you can put an **S** at the end of all of them. Even **MAN** (he mans the lifeboat),

WOMAN (to act like a woman or to staff with women) and **WIFE** (to become a wife or take a wife) are verbs which can have **S** after them (or 'take an **S**', as Scrabble players tend to say). In fact, nearly every noun and verb in the English language can take an **S**. Many of the smaller words take S, and not always because of their status as a noun or verb – **DI** is a noun but is plural already (plural of **DEUS**, a god), but you can have **DIS**, teenage slang meaning to disrespect.

> *Scrabble tip – Some unexpected words that take an* **S**
> *(i.e. they can have an* **S** *put at the end of them):*
>
> | | | |
> |---|---|---|
> | **EROTIC** | **ERRATIC** | **MALTED** |
> | **PRY** | **TELLY** | **TRILBY** |
> | **WICKED** | | |

Even a lot of words that end in **S** take an **S** – **PRINCES** (to give **PRINCESS**), **POSSES** (to give **POSSESS**), **BRAS** (to give **BRASS**), **NEEDLES** (to give **NEEDLESS**) and indeed **DIS** (to give **DISS**, to treat with contempt). **ZEBRAS** can become **ZEBRASS** (a cross between a zebra and an ass), and if you're ever in a game where **DEADLINE** is played, then someone makes it **DEADLINES**, you could well and truly flabbergast your opponent by turning that into **DEADLINESS**.

> *Scrabble facts – Don't forget that there are four* **S** *tiles in a set, so there's a reasonably high chance that you'll get one at some point in the game.*

Using your S

The relevance of all this to the **S** on your Scrabble rack is twofold. Firstly, if you can make a six-letter word with the other six letters, the chances are you'll be able to stick an **S** on the end of it and, you've got a seven-letter word. So you've only got six letters to worry about manipulating. That means, assuming no blanks or duplicates, you only have 720 different ways to arrange your tiles which, while it might sound quite a lot, is a lot easier than the 5,040 ways you can arrange seven different tiles.

Of course, you may have a seven-letter word with an **S** in it, but the **S** isn't at the end. For example, with a rack of **I L N O R S T**, it may only be after coming up with wrong 'uns like *litrons* and *trinols* that you finally sniff out **NOSTRIL**. However, it's worth putting your **S** at the end of the rack and thinking around the other six to start with, and only if that fails, should you need to be more imaginative.

Secondly, once you've found your bonus word, you have a high chance of being able to fit it in. What can match the desolation of working out a splendid seven and then not being able to get it down? But with all those other words already on the board, most of them taking an **S**, you will usually have a couple of positions onto which you can hook your brilliant bonus.

It is worth stressing that you should not necessarily hang onto an **S** until you can get a bonus with it. Its usefulness for hooking means you can often get a good score without using it in a bonus word. Watch especially for positions where you can get two words doubled with the addition of an **S**. Look at the board opposite with a Double Word square next to **FIRM**.

If you have an **S** in this position, you should be looking to make whatever word you can with it, and use it to turn **FIRM** into **FIRMS**. If you can get a high-scorer on the Double Letter square, so much the better. Something like **WRITS**, coming down to also make **FIRMS**, would score 44 (see board on the next page).

A good board for playing an **S**.

Using the **S** to get down **WRITS** scores 44.

To summarize, the **S** can:

- Allow you to play a word, hooking an existing word, and thus scoring for both.
- Increase your chance of finding a seven-letter word.
- Taking 1 and 2 together, it can increase your chance of finding a playable seven-letter word.

You should expect to score at least 20 for an **S**, preferably more than 25.

The two **S**s problem

If one **S** is good, it follows that two on your rack at the same time must be twice as good. Right? Wrong!

Why? Well, quite simply, two of anything on your rack tends to weaken it (leaving aside blanks, which we'll come to in the next chapter). It's all to do with those different combinations again – you have far fewer separate ways of arranging your letters if you have a duplicate.

Two **E**s are usually alright, because **E** is such a common letter in English. And two **S**s are certainly better than some other duplicates; the dreaded duplicate **V** or **U** are real killers. But a second **S** has basically lost its advantage of being an **S** – its essential 'essness' (no, not a valid word). If you put one **S** to one side, hoping to make a word with the other six letters, and then stick the **S** at the end of it to make a seven, what has happened is that your second **S** has turned into just another letter. You're not really very likely to pick the letters for **ZEBRASS**, and your opponent would be amazed if you got all four **S**s for **POSSESS**.

As it happens, the most common initial letter for a word in *Collins Scrabble Lists* is **S**, and by quite a long way. So yes, there are lots of words, many of them seven- and eight-letter words, that begin and end with an **S**. Then there are armies of words ending in –**ISES** and –**ISTS**.

So it's far from impossible to get a bonus word with two Ss. It's just not twice as easy as getting one with one S.

Generally, the thing to do with a duplicate S is play one, hooking it onto a word already on the board, making another word at the same time, preferably using your higher-scoring tiles – you should be getting the hang of it by now – and then you're still left with one S and your lower-scoring tiles with which, fingers crossed, to get a bonus next time.

S at the beginning

As well as being an 'end hook' (going on the end of a word), the S is frequently also a 'front hook'; which means that it can be placed at the front of a word to form another word. You can often put an S at the front of words beginning with:

C: **(S)CAM, (S)CAMP, (S)CABBY, (S)CANNER, (S)CURRIED,** and many more, including unusual words like **(S)CAMEL** and **(S)COPULATE.**

H: **(S)HOD, (S)HALL, (S)HATTER, (S)HEATH, (S)HELLFIRE** and, more surprisingly, **(S)HADDOCK** and **(S)HOOKS.**

L: **(S)LAP, (S)LINK, (S)LOUGH, (S)LIPPY, (S)LIGHTLY** and nice words like **(S)LOWDOWN** and **(S)LAUGHTER.**

P: **(S)PUD, (S)PRAY, (S)PRINT, (S)PRIEST, (S)PLATTER** and the more unexpected **(S)PINK** and **(S)PROD.**

T: **(S)TRAP, (S)TANNIC, (S)TICKER, (S)TAKEOUT** and **TATUS,** the plural of an old spelling of tattoo, converts rather pleasingly into **STATUS.**

Words beginning with **M**, **N**, **W** and even **Q** are also good to check for **S** front-hooks. And of course, like most other consonants, it will often go before a word starting with a vowel (**S-ADDER**, **S-EVEN**, **S-IRE**, **S-ODIUM**, **S-UNDRESS**). Add in exotica like **S-DEIGN** and **S-GRAFFITI** and you might almost start to think an **S** was as likely to go before a word as after it. It is, however, its power as an end hook that makes the **S** such a potent weapon to have on your rack.

HAVE A GO
CHALLENGE NO. 4

With the board position and rack shown below:

1. Can you find two seven-letter words – both fairly simple words ending in **S**?
2. Can you find one place where each fits on the board?
3. Can you see where you could play an eight-letter word (not ending in **S**) that would hit a Triple Word square?

Your rack is **A E L L R S U**

6 Using the blank

Sometimes a very inexperienced player will feel hard done by when they pick the blank, because it doesn't score anything. Wrong, wrong, wrong!

If you pick a blank, your heart should leap like a March hare on a trampoline. So long as there is an opening on the board somewhere, a blank should set you on your way to being able to play a bonus word, maybe not immediately, but reasonably soon.

Why? It's those combinations again. The larger the number of different ways you can form your rack into seven letters, the more likely it is that one of them will be a seven-letter word. We've already noted that a straightforward rack of seven different letters can be arranged 5,040 different ways. But six different letters plus a blank can be arranged in a massive 115,920 ways, counting the blank as each possible letter in each separate position. That's 23 times as many; picking a blank is like having 23 tickets in the lottery instead of just one.

> **Scrabble facts** – Don't forget that the blank has no value, whatever letter it is standing in for.

How to use the blank

You could try painstakingly working your way through all 115,920 combinations to find if you have a seven-letter word. At, say, 10 seconds per combination, that would take about 13½ days, assuming you don't stop for sleeping, eating or other essentials. Your opponent may get a tad restless. Happily, your brain will automatically shut out consideration of the vast number of these combinations that are obviously fruitless. In addition, the following will help you work at the challenge:

1 If some of your letters form a useful combination such as **–ING** or **–ATE**, put the blank with the other letters and see if any words suggest themselves. **G H I L N R ?** (**?** represents a blank) might look a bit of a mishmash. But make it **H L R ? + I N G** and it should immediately resolve itself into **HURLING**.

2 If there are no such handy combinations on your rack, go through the alphabet, making the blank each letter in turn. **D F I M N U ?** may not immediately look like anything, but once you try making the blank an **L**, **MINDFUL** might pop into your head.

3 Perhaps the blank will become the last letter in one of those useful combinations. **G H I L R U ?** also makes **HURLING**, even though you can't immediately isolate **–ING**.

4 You may be able to save a bit of time and mental energy by eliminating several possibilities for the blank:

   • If you have five consonants, one vowel and a blank, the blank is almost certainly going to have to be a vowel if you are using it to make a seven-letter word.

   • More obviously, with five bonus-friendly tiles (i.e. mainly one-pointers with a good vowel–consonant balance) plus a blank and a **Q**, there's really only one letter you need to think about making the blank. If you don't have a **U**, that's almost certainly what the blank is going to have to be if you are going for a bonus.

Play your blank with care

You must avoid the ultimate Scrabble crime of wasting your blank for a low score. Don't just stick it into a four- or five-letter word for a few points, even if you can't see anything else. Hold onto the blank and get rid of some of your more awkward tiles, even for a lower score this time round, and some bonus possibilities ought to start revealing themselves within one or two moves.

In club and tournament Scrabble, the blank will rarely be played other than in a bonus move, unless the blank is picked right at the end of the game, when it may be too late to knock the rest of the rack into shape or there may be nowhere to play a bonus.

You may also be able to use the blank to get a move as good as a bonus, even if not an actual one. Remember we talked about getting a **J**, **Q**, **X** or **Z** on a Premium Letter square, at the same time as getting the word on a Premium Word square. Such a move can easily score 60–70 points or more, and could be well worth using a blank for.

> *Scrabble tip* – *Do you ever feel the blank in the Scrabble bag? Mattel produce special tile sets for tournaments where every tile is smooth.*

As a general rule, you should be looking to score at least 50 for a blank.

Two blanks

Even some quite experienced club players claim to dislike getting two blanks at the same time. The mesmerizingly high number of different combinations that can be made throws some people into confusion, and they say they 'just can't think', or even, appropriately enough, 'go blank'. This is a bit like people who say that being rich doesn't make you happy. It may be true, but you wouldn't mind giving it a try anyway.

The fact is that with two blanks you should be well on your way to making a bonus, unless the board is extremely blocked. If you find a double blank difficult to cope with, try thinking of one of them as the most useful letter it could be (bearing in mind your other five tiles) if it was not a blank. With a rack of, say, **A A C I P ? ?**, given that you have three vowels, at least one of your blanks is going to be a consonant. So think of it as one of those one-point, bonus-friendly consonants like **N** or **T**, and words like **CAPTAIN** and **CAPITAL** should soon start suggesting themselves to you. If you have **H O R T X ? ?**, make the rack more manageable by calling one blank an **E**, and **EXHORTS** suddenly becomes much easier to find.

However, with a rack like that, you may be able to play your **X**, perhaps with one of the blanks, for around 40 points, and still have a good chance of the bonus next turn. Unless you can play **EXHORTS** (or whatever) for a real stonker of a score – I would suggest at least 80 – a rack with lots of goodies like that should be good for two high scores.

Never change a blank

Above all, never change a blank. Why give your opponent the chance of picking it later? The only possible time you might want to try breaking that rule is if you are over 100 behind, and thus need two bonuses to come back. You could try putting a blank back in the hope of picking it later and getting bonuses with both of them. But this is an unwise tactic – particularly as by changing you waste a turn and fall even further behind.

HAVE A GO
CHALLENGE NO. 5

What type of letter is the blank almost certainly going to be to form a seven-letter word?

Can you find the seven-letter word? And where would you play it?

Your rack is **B D O R R S ?**

7 Finding the bonus words

Once you have mastered (and I do mean mastered) the twos, started
learning some useful threes, lost your fear of **J**, **Q**, **X** and **Z**, and realized
the value of the **S** and the blank, the next step on your road to being an
accomplished Scrabble player is to be able to play bonus words; in other
words, play out all seven of your letters in one go for that lovely, satisfying,
game-changing, onlooker-impressing, opponent-shattering 50-point bonus.

Making bonus words

You may manage the occasional bonus now, but if you can get up to
playing a regular one per game, then two per game, you will soon see
your average score rocketing out of the sub-200 doldrums and into the
stratosphere of 300+ and even 400+ (based on a two-player game).

So how is it done? Essentially, there are two keys to playing bonuses
regularly: **managing your rack** and **knowing the words**. In this chapter
we will look first at the various ways of managing your rack and then at
how to form words through the use of **prefixes and suffixes** and by
creating **compound words**.

Rack management

It's not just knowing words, it's knowing the right words that counts.
There is no point in the random learning of seven-letter words. **PUPUNHA**,
MUNDIFY or **THRUTCH** may just show up on someone's rack somewhere
between now and the next millennium, but that's not the way to bet. Better
by far to get familiar with words which, on the balance of probabilities, will
come up on your rack with reasonable regularity.

Rack management essentially means knowing which letters to keep and which letters to get rid of to maximize your chances of a good score next time – preferably a bonus. Just as a good snooker player doesn't take a whack at the first ball he sees but tries to make sure he leaves himself an easy shot for next time, so should a Scrabble player have an eye to what he or she is storing up for the future.

Rack management: keep the right letters

The first thing to know when working out which letters to keep and which to play is the distribution of the tiles in a set. In other words, how many **A**s are there, how many **B**s, etc. Happily, many Scrabble boards actually list this distribution down one side of the board. We list them in Chapter 2. If your board doesn't, it's fairly easy to have a rough idea of how many of a particular letter are in the set by its point value:

> *Scrabble tip – Know the distribution of tiles in the set by point value.*
>
> | Point value | Number in set |
> | --- | --- |
> | 1 | 4–12 |
> | 2 | 3–4 |
> | 3–4 | 2 |
> | 5–10 | 1 |

Clearly, the fewer points a letter scores, the more there are of them. There are lots of the common letters to help you make words, but they don't score so much. There are fewer of the less common letters because they're harder to use, but they are worth more points.

This means a rack is going to tend towards having a lot of the one-point tiles: 68 of the 98 tiles (leaving aside the blanks) are worth one point.

So the best bonus words to learn must be the ones consisting wholly or mainly of one-point letters.

Rack management: one-point letters

So which are the one-point letters? There are 10 of them: the five vowels **A E I O U**, plus five consonants, **L N R S T**.

Are these the 10 commonest letters in the language? A statistical analysis of over a million words of English covering newspaper reports, scientific and religious writing and general fiction concluded that the most frequently used letters, in order, were: **E T A O I N S R H L**.

So nine of our 10 commonest letters in the Scrabble set agree with this study. The rogue interloper in the study is **H**, but its frequency can be explained by the number of short, very common words in which it appears:

THE	THAT	THIS	THESE	THOSE
HE	SHE	THEY	HIM	HER
THEM	HIS	HERS	THEIR	WHICH
WHAT	WHO	HOW	WHY	

Thus the letter **H** appears in a passage of written or spoken English much more often than it would in a random collection of unconnected words.

The letter **U**

So the missing letter from our 'Scrabble Top Ten', the **U**, presumably came 11th in the statistical survey? Actually, it came 13th, behind **D** and **C**.

So why are there so many **U**s in the Scrabble set? Scrabble's creator, Alfred Butts, decided on the number of each letter by counting the frequency with which each appeared in three newspapers, the *New York*

Times, the *Herald Tribune* and the *Evening Post*. But it seems clear that he must have made some judicious adjustments after his mammoth count. He would have had to iron out the **H** problem, for one. And he also realized that there had to be a reasonable number of **U**s so that players could play the **Q**. (**QI**, **QAT**, **QADI** and the other non-**U** words would not have been part of his thinking at that time.) Four **U**s would be enough to give a reasonable chance of shedding the awkward **Q**, but not so many that players would be overburdened with a letter which, apart from **Q** duty, is not particularly helpful.

Rack management: the right vowels

The vowels have a fairly clear hierarchy of usefulness. **E** is the biggie. It's difficult (far from impossible, but difficult) to get a bonus without an **E**. As you may have discovered yourself, it can be hard playing any good move without an **E**. **A** and **I** come next, about equally useful, closely followed by **O**. As the ideal vowel–consonant split is three vowels and four consonants, it follows that the vowels you want on your rack are **A E I**. Even though our million-word analysis placed **O** above **I**, experience in Scrabble shows that the **I** is easier to work with.

> *Scrabble tip – In Scrabble* **I** *is more useful than* **O**.
> *It can be used in lots of suffixes:*
> **–ING, –IER, –IEST, –ISE, –IZE, –ISM** *and* **–IST**.

So do you try to keep **A E I** on your rack, and play any **O** or **U** that you have? Maybe, but it's not always quite that simple.

How to manage duplicate vowels

The problem of duplicated letters can easily come to haunt you with vowels, especially the **A** and **I**. You don't want two of either of these letters on your rack, because comparatively few words have two **A**s or two **I**s in them. Yes, there are all the words ending in **–ING**, thus giving **AIMING**, **BOILING**, **CHIDING** and lots of others, or the **–IER** and **–IEST** words – **DIRTIER**, **FIERIER**, **GIDDIEST**, etc., and no doubt you can rattle off a dozen words off the top of your head with two **A**s as well. However, duplicates radically diminish the number of different ways you can arrange the letters on your rack, and that constricts the number of useful moves you can make.

Tracking the letters played

For this reason, it is always a good idea to keep track of how many **A**s and **I**s have been played. Let's say it's about halfway through the game, with about 45 or 50 letters on the board. There are six **A**s on the board and two **I**s. You also have one of each on your rack. You can see that you are far more likely to pick another **I** than another **A**, so it makes sense to play the **I** if you can, but not be so concerned about ditching the **A**.

> *Scrabble facts – The distribution of vowels in a set is:*
> *twelve* **E**s   *nine* **A**s   *nine* **I**s
> *eight* **O**s   *four* **U**s

This should not take precedence over any really good move you can make that involves keeping the **I** and playing the **A**. But, other things being equal, play the **I**. A choice between **BAD** and **BID**? Go for **BID**. Wondering about **CARP**? Perhaps with a judicious reshuffle you could make it **PRIG** instead.

If you play bridge or poker, you will know the value of remembering the cards that have been played or folded. In poker, you don't try for the third six to go with your pair if both the other sixes are gone. In bridge, the king of trumps must win a trick if the ace is gone. We are using the exact same principle here in Scrabble. You use your knowledge of what has already been played to help you predict what will happen next. Except it's easier in Scrabble because you don't need to remember – the 'discarded' letters are all there face up on the board in front of you, so all you need to do is count them. (You might not even need to do that – in a later chapter, we'll look at the concept of tile-tracking, which shows you at a glance how many of each letter are still to come.)

The **E**, as we have already seen, is a sufficiently useful letter that to hold two of them is no bad thing. And there are plenty of four-letter words with a double **O** in the middle if you want to get rid of a couple of **O**s – but four-letter words with two **A**s or two **I**s are considerably thinner on the ground. Of course, you don't need to get rid of both your duplicates to alleviate your problem, as you only need to play one – but there is a comfort in having those double-**O** words available if you need them.

So, we have the apparently contradictory situation that one **A** or one **I** on your rack is better than one **O**, because **A** and **I** are commoner letters, especially for bonuses. But two **O**s are better than two **A**s or two **I**s, because they're easier to get rid of in short words.

An example

It's halfway through a game, there are four **A**s, four **I**s and four **O**s to come, and you have one of each on your rack.

Do you play **BID**, **BAD** or **BOD**?

The answer is, probably, play **BOD**.

The extra strength of **A** and **I** over **O** just about overrides the fear of picking a duplicate. But much would depend on other factors.

For example, if you have –**TION** on your rack, is it worth holding this useful suffix and playing the A? It could be, but you need to be aware that –**TION** is mainly useful for eight-letter bonuses; there are not many seven-letter words ending in –**TION**. So don't build your hopes up of getting a –**TION** bonus unless there are places on the board where an eight-letter word is playable.

If you think this is all starting to sound a bit technical, well, you're right. But that's the trouble with Scrabble racks – there is not always a clear-cut answer. It's like walking through a wood. This path is more overgrown, that one is muddier, a third goes uphill, and the fourth one looks pretty but there's a strange growling noise coming from its vicinity. Which one do you take? Hitting on the right one is a mixture of experience, common sense, instinct and luck.

Conclusion

We have established in general that **E** is the best vowel, **A** and **I** come next, **O** a little behind but with some points in its favour, and **U** the least useful. But even the humble **U** can be worth hanging onto if it is towards the end of the game and the **Q** hasn't appeared yet, especially if there are no handy places to slot in a **QI** or a **QAT**. So the distribution of vowels in Scrabble turns out to be about right. Well done, Alfred Butts!

Rack management: the right consonants

So what about consonants? Remember the one-point tiles, **L N R S T**. Holding on to these and discarding the rest is generally the quickest way to a bonus word. But as always, there are complications.

Below and on the next page we will consider each of these one-point consonants in turn.

The letter **L**

Of these five consonants, **L** is unquestionably the least useful. It should really be worth one and a half points. Hang on to it if you like but have no qualms about playing it away if you have a good move in which to play it.

The letter S

The **S** is a special case which we have already discussed in Chapter 5. If your rack is your afternoon tea-break, the **S** is a cream cake – great to have, but two are no better than one and might leave you feeling sick.

The letter N

The **N** is a common letter and is useful for forming words with –**ING**, –**TION** and –**SION**. But a word of warning about the **N** – it's a terrible letter for beginning words with. Try this little experiment: take your dictionary or *Collins Scrabble Lists*, and hold the '**N**' section between your thumb and forefinger. Look how skimpy it is. There are more words beginning with **W** than beginning with **N**. So if you have an **N** and you're trying to use it to start an eight-letter word for a bonus, my advice is – try something else, fast.

The letter R

Now, how about the **R**? Another useful letter, but again there's a catch. The **R** really needs an **E** to give it much value. It comes into its own because of the large number of words with the prefix **RE**–, or the suffix –**ER** (whether in its agent noun sense, e.g. **COUNTER**, **BUILDER**, or as a comparative of an adjective, e.g. **BLACKER**, **NEEDIER**). And it will not have escaped your notice that the one letter in both **RE**– and –**ER**, apart from **R**, is **E**. So if you don't have an **E**, and there aren't so many left that you're likely to pick one any time soon, don't bust a gut to hold on to an **R**.

The letter T

Which leaves the **T**. I am a **T** fan – apart from a blank, **S** or **E**, no letter gives me more comfort to hold on my rack than a **T**. The only trouble is, the statistics don't back up my enthusiasm as far as seven-and eight-letter words are concerned – the **N** and the **R** are slightly better, because of all those –**ING**s, **RE**–s, and –**ER**s. But that may be the point – the **T** is not dependent on specific other letters to make it useful, and my gut feeling is that its versatility makes it more valuable. A duplicate **T** is also far less of a handicap than a duplicate **N** or **R**. Cherish your **T**s, try not to play them unless you have no reasonable alternative, and a fair percentage of them will help you on the way to that elusive bonus.

I could analyse my games and try to produce statistics to back this up, but the trouble is that it would be something of a self-fulfilling prophecy. If I (generally) hold onto a **T** until I can make a bonus word with it, then I will obviously be able to count my bonuses and announce triumphantly that 50 per cent of them (or whatever) have a **T** in them, which wouldn't prove anything. But the **T** is a cheerful, sociable letter that will fit in with pretty much any rack it finds itself on, so if it knocks on your door, invite it in and make it comfortable. More often than not, it will reward your hospitality.

Rack management: the right balance

It goes without saying that if you've got a rack of **L N R S S T T** or **A E E I O O U**, then you haven't got a bonus. In fact, you haven't got much of a move at all. It's essential to maintain a balance of vowels and consonants, and we will look at what this means on the next page.

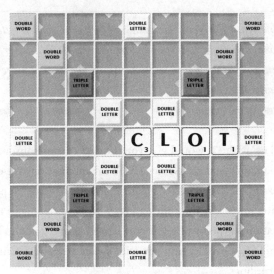

The right balance: your rack is **F I L N O U W**

An example

Let's say your opponent has started the game with **CLOT**, and your rack is as shown. Your first thought might be to play **FLOWN** through the **O**. That would get the high-scoring **F** on a Triple Letter square and net you an acceptable 21. But look what you've left yourself with on your rack: **I O U**. You may well pick at least two vowels among your four replacement tiles, leaving you with a vowel-heavy rack and little hope of a decent score next time.

You could still play **FLOWN**, but using the **L** on the board rather than the **O**. That only gets you 16 points, but leaves you with a more acceptable **I L U**. Still a bit too vowelly – ideally, if playing four tiles, you want to leave yourself two consonants and a vowel.

FLOUT, using the **T**, would give you the desired two-consonants, one-vowel outcome, and also scores 16. The main disadvantage of **FLOUT** is that **O** next to the Triple Letter square; although you have to play your own game and not worry too much about what your opponent might have. On this occasion the pesky blighter only needs a **Z** and an **O** up his or her sleeve to score 65 points, leaving you with a disheartening deficit at this stage of proceedings.

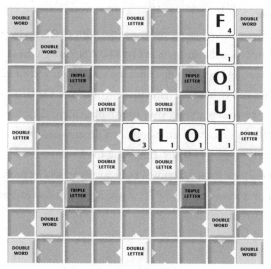

FLOUT scores 16,
but leaves a Triple Letter square next to the **O**.

Remembering that you should also be trying for **parallel** rather than **crosswise** plays, you might try **FOWL**. Not bad, scoring 18 points, though you are left with two vowels and one consonant. Pity about the **L** on the Double Letter square, rather than a higher-scoring letter. Hang on – how about **WOLF** in the same position? Now you score 21, the same as for **FLOWN**, and a more acceptable leave of **I N U**. (Scrabble players refer to the letters left on their rack after a move as the '*leave*'.)

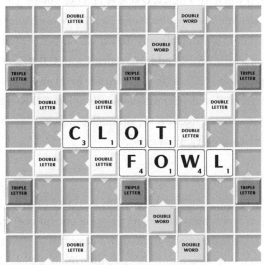

Playing **FOWL** in parallel is another option – and **WOLF** performs even better.

As so often in Scrabble, there is no clear-cut answer. **WOLF** and **FLOUT** both have something to recommend them, and personally I would go for **WOLF**. But they're both a big improvement on **FLOWN**, because of the better leave – we have given ourselves a better chance of a balanced rack for our next move.

Rack management: keep letters that go together

It's not just a case of keeping **A E I** and **N R S T** and maintaining a good vowel–consonant balance. Often you'll have to keep some other letters as well – you may not have many of **A E I N R S T**, so you have to decide what else to offload. Again, much will depend on what good scores are available – never lose sight of the fact that that is the object of the exercise. But it will often be worth accepting a less than optimal score to give yourself that all-important optimal leave. If you have a rack **C D G K W** and two vowels, you don't want to leave yourself with incompatible letters like **G K W**, which are unlikely to combine together in a profitable way next time. Far better to play **G W**, probably along with a vowel, and leave yourself with **C D K**, a much happier combination, especially if you draw (or already have) an **E** to go with them.

Some Scrabble players refer to combinations like **C D K** as having better synergy than ones like **G K W**, although others just say that the letters go together, which is every bit as good.

Strategy and rack management

One of the most difficult things in Scrabble is when you know you're close to a seven-letter bonus but you haven't quite got one (or can't quite find it if you have). You are loath to play more than one or two of your tiles, because you don't want to break up a promising combination, such as –**ERING** or –**NIEST**. But that means you are scoring only a handful of points, while your opponent may be forging ahead with 20s and 30s. After three attempts, you may finally get your bonus for, say, 65 points, only to find that while you were scoring six or eight at a time, your opponent notched up 75 points altogether and you are no better off.

So what are we saying here? Do you or don't you hang onto a **A E I N R S T** combination like **A E N T**, or a suffix like –**ISH**? Do you just check to see if they can help you make a seven-letter word if you have them on your rack at the time, but if they don't, just play what you can for a decent score? Or do you hoard them, in the hope that next shot you will be able to put down that satisfying, opponent-demoralizing bonus?

There is no easy answer. Among the things to take into account are:

1 *The score*
   If you are appreciably behind, you may have no alternative but to go for a bonus.
   If you're ahead, try to keep your score moving along and don't worry so much about bonus-hunting.

2 *The state of the board*
   Are there places to play a bonus word if you do get one?

3 *Are there bonus letters left to come?*
   There is little point in trying for a bonus if the unseen letters are mainly **O**s, **U**s and higher-scoring consonants.

Remember that the extra 50 points from a bonus gives you such a powerful propulsion of points that it is worth devoting a lot of time to learning how to get them. If your rack is even starting to look as if it might make a bonus, and the board has openings or spaces where you can create openings, then it has to be worth considering.

Prefixes and suffixes

You should now be aware of the need to hold on to a reasonable balance of vowels and consonants and to keep the letters **N R S T** and **A E I** (think of the word **RETAINS**), as long as you are scoring reasonably in the meantime. When you keep other letters, you are trying to make sure they are compatible with each other. But the seven-letter words are unlikely to just turn up on your rack with all the letters in the right order. You still have to sort the letters out.

So how do you find the seven-letter word that may be sitting on your rack and earn those 50 lovely bonus points? The first things to check for are **prefixes** and **suffixes**.

Suffixes

Remember that some of these suffixes can do a double duty. **–ER** can form an *agent noun* (**BUILDER** from **BUILD**) or a *comparative adjective* (**SHORTER** from **SHORT**). **–ISH** can go after an adjective or noun to mean 'somewhat' or 'somewhat like' (**WARMISH, HAWKISH**). If you have an **F**, you could also try and catch one of the many available **FISH** which may be swimming around, such as **CATFISH, DOGFISH** or the rather unimaginatively named **FINFISH**.

Be careful about –ING

A quick word of warning about **–ING**. It's very tempting to hang onto these letters if you get them, come what may, in the expectation that they are bound to combine with almost any other four letters to form a seven-letter word. Well, sometimes they will and sometimes they won't, but it doesn't happen as often as you might think. In the meantime you are effectively trying to play with only your other four letters, drastically minimizing your potential score. And if and when you do get an **–ING** word, the double-consonant **–NG** can make it difficult to fit into a parallel play, so you may well not be able to get it down on the board.

Prefixes

The kings of the prefix world are **RE–** and **UN–**. A quick glance through the **RE–** and **UN–** sections of *Collins Scrabble Lists* might suggest that you can put either of these two pairs of letters before almost any word. You will quickly be disabused of this notion if you start trying to do so during a game. There are many, many words, some of which look perfectly reasonable, that cannot be formed in this way.

> *Scrabble tip – Not all* **RE–** *words are valid, even if you think they look right. You CANNOT play:*
> **RECLAMP   RECOACH   RESLUMP   RESTAND**
> **RETRICK**
> *any of which look as feasible as some words which are valid, such as:*
> **REVICTUAL   RESPLICE**
> **REEDIFY** *(hyphen not compulsory).*

Remember, Scrabble players didn't write *Collins Scrabble Lists*, lexicographers did. They will be able to cite examples of usage for all the words in their dictionary, and have excluded those for which they could find no examples. Fine, but it doesn't help you much when you're trying to work out whether to risk **REHAPPEN** or **UNSEXY** (the latter is valid, the former not).

> *Scrabble tip – Not all* **UN**– *words are valid either.*
> *The* Collins Scrabble Lists *does NOT allow:*
> **UNLIGHT   UNDARK   UNRUNG   UNHAIRY   UNSAD**
> *but does approve of:*
> **UNBRIGHT   UNHEARSE   UNHONEST   UNMELLOW**

So **UN**– and **RE**– are useful to remember, and well worth putting to one side of your rack to see whether they'll help you towards a bonus, but the frequency with which they can be used makes it all the more heartbreaking when they let you down when you need them most. There are lots of other common prefixes which can ease your path towards that elusive seven-letter word.

> *Scrabble tip – Watch out for these prefixes to help you towards a bonus word:*
>
> | PRE– | PRO– | ANTI– | DIS– | MIS– | OUT– | OVER– |
> |------|------|-------|------|------|------|-------|
> | DE– | EN– | IN– | CON– | SUB– | UP– | |

Using S

Apart from prefixes and suffixes, how else can we discover seven-letter words on our rack? We have covered the obvious one of words ending in **S** in Chapter 5. If you have an **S**, always pop it to the end of your rack, and see if your other six letters can make a six-letter word that your **S** might go on the end of to make a seven.

Compound words

Something else to watch for is **compound words**. This can often pay dividends even if you have higher-scoring letters on your rack. Does your rack divide into a three-letter word and a four-letter word? If so, they just might combine to form a seven. There are lots of examples:

> **PAYBACK**   **AIRLINE**   **MANHUNT**   **FOOTPAD**   **SEAFOOD**
>
> **REDCOAT**   **SUNTRAP**   **WARSHIP**   **HATBAND**   **KEYHOLE**

This technique may lead you to an eight-letter word (using a letter on the board) giving you to a 4–4, 3–5 or 5–3 compound word:

> **AIRTIGHT**   **WORMWOOD**   **BLUEBIRD**
>
> **PAYCHECK**   **CAUSEWAY**

Always look at your letters in as many different ways as you can. A word with a **Q** doesn't have to begin with a **Q**. Words can begin with vowels, or end with vowels other than **E**.

A bonus-word challenge

Try and unravel these 20 teasers using the words shown below:

Five take unexpected letters before them to form other words.

Five take unexpected letters after them.

*Five end with **A, I, O** or **U**.*

*And five have a **J, Q, X** or **Z**, but where it comes in the word is up to you
to discover.*

SIPRAIN	RAJTHING	CANTHEN	AIMSTRAP
QUARPET	THRIVEON	FLYWAUL	SHEISVAL
FILMNAG	IPLOTSEX	AIHOOTS	DRAWPLOY
AACEHUT	RUEPHONE	ZELEGAL	PLUMTILE
IMAPLOD	HATEDEER	ILOVAIR	ZREFEREE

Some will be compound words or will use prefixes or suffixes.
The answers are given at the back of the book.

When you've got them, work out which 10 have the unexpected 'hooks' –
and see if you can find them. For example, if the answer was **BRIDGES**, the
hook would be **ABRIDGES**. For a hook at the end, **ELEVATOR** would
become **ELEVATORY** (as well as the obvious **ELEVATORS**).

How to look for bonus words

The only other advice I can give in spotting bonus words is simply to look for them. Obvious, I know – but it's easy to get into the habit of playing that reasonable move for 20 points or so, or that word which will leave you a perfectly balanced and compatible rack, while all the time the seven-letter word is hiding in there somewhere. The more you play, the more you will develop a feel for whether a rack is likely to contain a bonus.

Have a look at these racks:

A C D E H I R   A B I N O P T   A E L M N S V

E E F G L O R   A E I N O S T

First, without trying to work out what the seven-letter words might be, decide which combinations are likely to make a seven-letter word. Then, try and figure out the words. Let's look at them one at a time:

A C D E H I R

- The **C** and **H** might go together.
- And there's an **RE/ER**, in fact an **IER**, with other possibilities like **ED** and **IC**. **CHADIER**, **DACHIER** – nothing there.
- **CHAIDER**, **REDAICH** – the **RE** and **ER** don't appear to be much help.
- Maybe **IC** at the end – **HERADIC**? No, but a usable **L** on the board would give **HERALDIC**.
- A compound, perhaps – **ICEHARD**, **HARDICE**? **ICEHARD** sounds feasibly poetic but I haven't actually seen it anywhere, so it's a big risk.
- Finally, with the simple expedient of trying **ED** at the end to see if there might be a nice, simple past tense, and keeping our compatible **CH** together, we find the answer – **CHAIRED**.

A B I N O P T

- There is a **TION** in there but the only way the other three letters might go with them is **BAPTION** – not a word.
- No compounds suggest themselves.
- Nothing ending with **ANT**.
- The **ANTI** prefix likewise leads nowhere, unless someone who doesn't like dancing could be **ANTIBOP** – which is getting into the realms of fantasy.
- **BIOPTAN** sounds vaguely scientific but that doesn't make it a word.
- Finally, we correctly conclude that there is no seven-letter word here.

A E L M N S V

- Like **A B I N O P T**, it has five one-point tiles.
- It has an **S**, and both **MAN** and **MEN**.
- Any six-letter words from **A E L M N V** that the **S** might go after? **MALVEN**, **VELMAN**, **MENVAL** – all rubbish.
- **ELSV** doesn't combine with **MAN**, nor **ALSV** with **MEN**.
- The **A E L M N S** make a nice start and would go with various other letters to form a seven, but the **V** fouls things up – once again, regretfully, no seven-letter word.

E E F G L O R

- Not too promising on the face of it.
- **E F G L O** doesn't match up with **RE** or **ER** – **GEFOLER**, **REFLOGE**? Not a chance.
- **GOLFER** is in there but we have an **E** left over – still, it could be worth playing if we can get it on at least a Double Word for 20 or so.
- Any compounds? **EELFROG**? **LOGFREE**? **FOREGEL**? Hang on – **FORELEG**. The 4–3 split, using the fairly common **FORE** prefix, brings us to the seven-letter word.

- We got there mainly by technique, but with just that last little mental jump to finish the job.

A E I N O S T

- Now this looks good. Six of our **RETAINS** letters, and the seventh is a fairly acceptable **O**.
- A slight excess of vowels, but we have an S and there are prefixes and suffixes galore: –(I)EST, –ATE, –ISE, –TION, –SION, IN–, EN–, ANTI–.
- So what's the word? Well, there is one, but you could probably shuffle your tiles for ever and you wouldn't find it. It's **ATONIES**, the plural of **ATONY**, which means lack of muscle tone. It's an awkward, obscure word which not one person in a hundred will come across outside the confines of a Scrabble board. But **ATONY** is in *Collins Scrabble Lists*, and since the rule used in compiling *Collins Scrabble Lists* is that all nouns have a plural, that means **ATONIES** gets in as well.

Learning bonus words

And that brings us on to one more method of getting bonuses. It might not sound much fun, it might not be your idea of the spirit of a game, but there are many words which will keep coming up on your rack because they are composed of the common letters, and you just have to learn them. Sometimes games do require a bit of work. Ask a chess player who's memorized 50 standard openings up to the 20th move. Ask a footballer who's just completed a punishing two-hour training session in a downpour.

So the next two chapters will cut through the tips, techniques and strategies, and quite simply give you a whole batch of seven- and eight-letter words which, if you can learn them, will help you play bonus after bonus and really get your game moving up through the gears. You won't learn them all today, or tomorrow, but make a start, and come back to them as often as you can and learn a few more. You learnt the twos (or I hope you did) and some of the threes. You may well find sevens and eights easier because the words have a more familiar structure and may just seem less unlikely. It's a bit of a blow to the ego to be told there are so many two- and three-letter words you don't know, but it's easier to accept the existence of these longer words which you have never come across.

The words are divided into logical groups, and the lists are not exhaustive; many others could have been included, but at this stage you would be wise to concentrate on a manageable number. When a combination of seven or eight letters makes more than one word, these are sometimes shown, but not always. Even when more than one word is shown, there may be others with the same letters. But what is there is plenty to be getting on with. So make yourself a nice cup of tea, get your brain in gear, and start the next chapter.

8 Some seven-letter lists

Seven-letter words not only get you bonus scores, but they also help open up the board. You know now that, where possible and where it doesn't prevent you from getting a worthwhile score, you keep the letters **N R S T** and **A E I** to help you towards getting a bonus word.

The letters **A E I N R S T** make several seven-letter words:

RETAINS	**RETINAS**	**NASTIER**
STAINER	**RETSINA**	**STEARIN**

There are more, but they are rather obscure, and that selection should be enough to enable you to play a bonus on all but the most blocked of boards. The good news is that if you've got any six of the **R E T A I N S** letters and one other, you've probably got a bonus already.

'6 + 1' lists

These lists give all the seven-letter words that can be formed by adding one letter to a particular combination of six letters. Club players will learn these '6 + 1' lists so that once they have six of the seven letters, they can mentally flick through the appropriate list and come up with the bonus word. It's well worthwhile getting to grips with these lists, so they have been set out here for you.

> ***Scrabble facts** – Statistically, the seven-letter word you are most likely to pick out of a standard bag of tiles is **OTARINE**, the adjective from **OTARY**. An otary is any member of the seal family with ears.*

Often a combination will make more than one word, but I haven't included every anagram, and a couple of less likely combinations have been excluded. But there are plenty of words for you to get to grips with, and familiarising yourself with them will dramatically increase the number of bonuses you play. The lists start with **A E I N R S +** and shows the words that can be made by adding particular letters. Other examples follow on.

A E I N R S +

C	ARSENIC	CERASIN	
D	SANDIER	SARDINE	
F	INFARES	SERAFIN	
G	SEARING	REGAINS	
H	HERNIAS	ARSHINE	
I	SENARII		
J	INJERAS		
K	SNAKIER		
L	NAILERS	RENAILS	
M	REMAINS	SEMINAR	
N	INSANER	INSNARE	
O	ERASION		
P	PANIERS	RAPINES	
R	SIERRAN	SNARIER	
S	SARNIES	ARSINES	
T	RETAINS	RETINAS	NASTIER
	STAINER	RETSINA	STEARIN
V	RAVINES	AVENIRS	

AEINRT+

B	ATEBRIN		
C	CERTAIN	NACRITE	
D	TRAINED	DETRAIN	
E	RETINAE	TRAINEE	
F	FAINTER	FENITAR	
G	TEARING	GRANITE	
H	HAIRNET	INEARTH	
I	INERTIA		
J	NARTJIE	JANTIER	
K	KERATIN		
L	LATRINE	RELIANT	
M	MINARET	RAIMENT	
N	ENTRAIN	TRANNIE	
O	OTARINE		
P	PAINTER	REPAINT	
R	TRAINER	RETRAIN	
S	RETAINS	RETINAS	NASTIER
	STAINER	RETSINA	STEARIN
T	NATTIER	NITRATE	
U	URINATE	TAURINE	
W	TAWNIER	TINWARE	

A	ENTASIA	TAENIAS	
B	BESAINT	BASINET	
C	CANIEST	CINEAST	
D	STAINED	INSTEAD	
E	ETESIAN		
F	FAINEST	NAIFEST	
G	TEASING	INGATES	
H	SHEITAN	STHENIA	
I	ISATINE		
J	JANTIES	TAJINES	
K	INTAKES	TANKIES	
L	ENTAILS	SALIENT	
M	INMATES	MAINEST	
N	INANEST	STANINE	
O	ATONIES		
P	SAPIENT	PANTIES	
R	RETAINS	RETINAS	NASTIER
	STAINER	RETSINA	STEARIN
S	NASTIES	SESTINA	
T	INSTATE	SATINET	
U	AUNTIES	SINUATE	
V	VAINEST	NATIVES	
W	TAWNIES	AWNIEST	
X	ANTISEX	SEXTAIN	
Z	ZANIEST	ZEATINS	

A	ASTERIA	ATRESIA	
B	BAITERS	REBAITS	
C	RACIEST	STEARIC	
D	TIRADES	ASTRIDE	
E	AERIEST	SERIATE	
F	FAIREST		
G	GAITERS	STAGIER	
H	HASTIER	SHERIAT	
I	AIRIEST	IRISATE	
K	ARKITES	KARITES	
L	RETAILS	REALIST	
M	MISRATE	SMARTIE	
N	RETAINS	RETINAS	NASTIER
	STAINER	RETSINA	STEARIN
O	OARIEST	OTARIES	
P	PARTIES	PIRATES	
R	TARRIES	ARTSIER	
S	SATIRES	TIRASSE	
T	ARTISTE	TASTIER	
V	VASTIER	TAIVERS	
W	WAITERS	WARIEST	

A	ANESTRA		
B	BANTERS		
C	CANTERS	TRANCES	
D	STANDER	ENDARTS	
E	EASTERN	NEAREST	
G	STRANGE	GARNETS	
H	ANTHERS	THENARS	
I	RETAINS	RETINAS	NASTIER
	STAINER	RETSINA	STEARIN
K	TANKERS	RANKEST	
L	RENTALS	ANTLERS	
M	SMARTEN	MARTENS	
N	TANNERS		
O	SENATOR	TREASON	
P	PARENTS	ENTRAPS	
R	ERRANTS	RANTERS	
S	SARSNET	TRANSES	
T	NATTERS	RATTENS	
U	NATURES	SAUNTER	
V	SERVANT	TAVERNS	
W	WANTERS	STRAWEN	
Y	TRAYNES		

A	ARTISAN	TSARINA	
B	BRISANT		
C	NARCIST		
D	INDARTS		
E	RETAINS	RETINAS	NASTIER
	STAINER	RETSINA	STEARIN
G	RATINGS	STARING	
H	TARNISH		
L	RATLINS		
M	MARTINS		
N	RATIONS	AROINTS	
P	SPIRANT	SPRAINT	
Q	QINTARS		
S	STRAINS	INSTARS	
T	TRANSIT	STRAINT	
U	NUTRIAS		

A	RETAINS	RETINAS	NASTIER
	STAINER	RETSINA	STEARIN
C	CISTERN	CRETINS	
D	TINDERS		
E	ENTRIES	TRENISE	
F	SNIFTER		
G	RESTING	STINGER	
H	HINTERS		
K	STINKER	TINKERS	
L	LINTERS	SNIRTLE	
M	MINSTER	ENTRISM	
N	INTERNS	TINNERS	
O	STONIER	ORIENTS	
P	NIPTERS	PTERINS	
S	INSERTS	SINTERS	
T	TINTERS	ENTRIST	
U	UNITERS	NUTSIER	
V	INVERTS	STRIVEN	
W	WINTERS	TWINERS	
Y	SINTERY		

You may have noticed that **A I N R S T** is by far the shortest of these lists, handicapped as it is by the lack of an **E**. The **A E I N R T** list is not nearly so held back by the absence of an **S**. **A I N R S T** does, however, have the saving grace of being the only one to combine with a **Q**.

Players who are used to dealing with these lists tend to refer to them as the **RETAIN** list, the **SARNIE** list, the **SANTER** list and so on. Note that **SANTER** isn't actually a word, it's just a convenient way of referring to the list. 'The **ASTERN** list' doesn't seem to have caught on, for some reason.

There are other lists which are just as good. **RAINED** and **TORIES** are both excellent six-letter combinations for forming sevens, as you can see below.

R A I N E D +

A	ARANEID	
B	BRAINED	BANDIER
C	CAIRNED	DANCIER
D	DRAINED	DANDIER
F	FRIANDE	
G	READING	GRAINED
H	HANDIER	
I	DENARII	
M	ADERMIN	INARMED
N	NARDINE	
O	ANEROID	
P	PARDINE	
R	DRAINER	RANDIER
S	SARDINE	SANDIER
T	TRAINED	DETRAIN
U	UNAIRED	URANIDE
V	INVADER	RAVINED

A	OARIEST	OTARIES
B	ORBIEST	SORBITE
C	EROTICS	TERCIOS
D	EDITORS	STEROID
E	EROTISE	
F	FORTIES	FOISTER
G	GOITRES	GORIEST
H	HOISTER	SHORTIE
I	RIOTISE	
K	ROKIEST	
L	LOITERS	TOILERS
M	MOISTER	EROTISM
N	STONIER	ORIENTS
O	SOOTIER	OORIEST
P	RIPOSTE	ROPIEST
R	ROISTER	RIOTERS
S	STORIES	ROSIEST
T	STOITER	
U	TOUSIER	OURIEST
V	TORSIVE	
W	OWRIEST	TOWSIER

There are lots of these '6 + 1' lists that are worth knowing, and, once you are familiar with a few, some of the seven-letter words will be known to you already from previous lists. For instance, **R A I N E D** + **T** is the same as **R E T A I N** + **D** (**TRAINED**, **DETRAIN** and the more unusual **ANTIRED**), while **T O R I E S** + **N** equals **I N T E R S** + **O** (**STONIER**, **ORIENTS** and a couple of others).

> *Scrabble facts* – *Among the least likely sevens to show up on your rack, most of which need one or even both blanks, are* **PIZAZZY** *(full of* **pizazz**), **MUUMUUS** *(loose dress worn in Hawaii),* **JAZZMAN** *and* **ZYZZYVA** *(American weevil).*

Lists by prefixes and suffixes

Another way of listing words is by going back to those prefixes and suffixes. It's useful to learn some of the more likely sevens that could come up with each of them.

Selection of seven-letter words listed by prefix

ANTI:	ANTIFLU, ANTIFOG, ANTILOG, ANTIPOT, ANTISAG
CON:	CONFEST, CONGREE, CONGRUE, CONSEIL, CONURES
DE:	DEALATE, DEBRIDE, DEGAMES, DEMEANE, DEPAINT
EN:	ENARMED, ENFLAME, ENLIGHT, ENRANKS, ENTAYLE
IN:	INDENES, INFAUST, INHUMER, INQUERE, INTURNS
MIS:	MISDRAW, MISEDIT, MISKEEP, MISMATE, MISPART
OUT:	OUTDARE, OUTEARN, OUTLAND, OUTPORT, OUTWEAR
OVER:	OVERAGE, OVERDOG, OVERHOT, OVERMEN, OVERWET
PRE:	PREAGED, PRECOOL, PRENAME, PREORAL, PRERACE
PRO:	PROETTE, PROLANS, PROLINE, PRONAOS, PROOTIC
SUB:	SUBAREA, SUBDEAN, SUBHEAD, SUBLINE, SUBRENT
UP:	UPCOILS, UPDRIED, UPLEAPT, UPSTARE, UPTRAIN

There are too many **RE–** and **UN–** words to give just five examples, so we have listed almost an alphabet of words for each one.

Seven-letter words starting with RE–

REARISE	REINTER	REQUITE
REBREED	REJONES	RERAILS
RECHEAT	REKEYED	RESPELL
REDREAM	RELABEL	RETUNDS
REENDOW	REMERGE	REUNIFY
REFLAGS	RENESTS	REVOTES
REGRATE	REOILED	REWAKEN
REHEARS	REPURES	REZONES

Seven-letter words starting with UN–

UNALIVE	UNJADED	UNROOTS
UNBARES	UNKINGS	UNSOBER
UNCAPED	UNLEADS	UNTENTY
UNDEALT	UNMITRE	UNURGED
UNEAGER	UNNOBLE	UNVISOR
UNFAIRS	UNOFTEN	UNWATER
UNGIRDS	UNPAINT	UNYOKES
UNHEALS	UNQUIET	UNZONED
UNIDEAL		

Some of the **UN–** words in particular are fairly unexpected; it's a bit hard to see how you can **UNWATER** or **UNPAINT** something, and isn't the opposite of **NOBLE IGNOBLE**? It might seem from looking at these lists that you can put **UN** at the front of almost anything, and maybe **RE** as well. You can't. It's a hard lesson that all Scrabble players learn sooner or later.

But back to our lists, and where there are prefixes, can suffixes be far behind? Here are some words from those useful suffixes which we looked at previously.

ABLE:	CITABLE, FRIABLE, HIDABLE, SEEABLE, TUNABLE
AGE:	CORDAGE, LISTAGE, PEONAGE, PIERAGE, SPINAGE
ANT:	FLOTANT, ITERANT, PERSANT, REPTANT, SEALANT
ATE:	CITRATE, DEALATE, EPILATE, PELTATE, SERIATE
ENT:	CONCENT, EXIGENT, FULGENT, MORDENT, PENDENT
IER:	BALDIER, HERBIER, LINTIER, RUNTIER, SEDGIER
IEST:	AWNIEST, BABIEST, LINIEST, MINIEST, RICIEST
ISE/IZE:	ADONISE/IZE, EROTISE/IZE, IRONISE/IZE, POETISE/IZE, RIOTISE/IZE
ISH:	ALUMISH, DEAFISH, FLEMISH, MAIDISH, PIGFISH
IST:	ABLEIST, DADAIST, ELOGIST, LEFTIST, TUBAIST
LESS:	BITLESS, EGOLESS, HATLESS, NAPLESS, TIPLESS
LIKE:	BEELIKE, FATLIKE, NETLIKE, RATLIKE, TINLIKE
LY:	DATEDLY, GAUNTLY, OBESELY, STAIDLY, USEABLY
MAN/MEN:	BEDEMAN/MEN, GUDEMAN/MEN, LINEMAN/MEN, ODDSMAN/MEN, TOPSMAN/MEN
NESS:	ALLNESS, FARNESS, HOTNESS, OUTNESS, SHINESS
TION:	ELUTION, ENATION, LECTION, PACTION, RECTION

It's worth repeating what was said in the last chapter that the four-letter prefixes and suffixes (or affixes, as they're collectively known) often don't make quite as many sevens as you might think. **TION**, for example, is not great for ending seven-letter words. You really need to have scope on the board to make an eight-letter word to get the best out of these slightly longer affixes.

There are too many –**ING** and –**ED** words to make it worth picking out five examples of each, so here are a few –**ING** sevens that can take **S**.

BOLTING(S)	HALTING(S)	SEALING(S)
COOKING(S)	HOSTING(S)	SEELING(S)
DANCING(S)	KEEPING(S)	SHARING(S)
FOILING(S)	LIMPING(S)	STEWING(S)
GASPING(S)	NESTING(S)	TILTING(S)
GETTING(S)	PIECING(S)	WANTING(S)
GREYING(S)	RUSTING(S)	

'High probability' seven-letter words

There are a lot of 'high probability' seven-letter words, so-called because they are composed mainly of common letters and are therefore more likely to come up on your rack. However, they don't fit easily into any of our categories such as containing six of the **R E T A I N S** letters, or being formed from a prefix or suffix. Here are some sevens, only a few of which you are likely to be familiar with, but which are well worth knowing, and which we haven't managed to shoehorn into previous lists (or in one or two cases we have, but this list has some anagrams of them). We'll start with some with four or more vowels, since it's nice to have a few at your fingertips for when you have more vowels than would otherwise be ideal.

Seven-letter words with five vowels

AEOLIAN	ETAERIO	OLEARIA	TAENIAE

Seven-letter words with four vowels (with anagrams grouped together)

ADONISE/ANODISE/SODAINE		AEDILES/DEISEAL
AILERON/ALERION/ALIENOR		AIRDATE/TIARAED
AIRLINE	ALIENER	ALUNITE
AMNIOTE	ANEROID	ANISOLE
ANTLIAE	ARANEID	ARENOSE
ARENOUS	ATELIER/REALTIE	
AUDIENT	AUDILES/DEASIUL	
DARIOLE	DEASOIL/ISOLEAD	
ELATION/TOENAIL		ELOINER
EMAILED/LIMEADE		EROTICA
GOATIER	GODETIA	INEDITA
IODATES/TOADIES		ISOLATE
LEIPOAS	LINEATE	MORAINE/
		ROMAINE
NIOBATE	OCEANID	ORDINEE
ORIGANE	RADIATE	RAINOUT
REGINAE	ROADIES/SOREDIA	
ROSEATE	TROELIE	URALITE

Seven-letter words with four or five consonants (with anagrams grouped together)

AGRISED   AIDLESS/DEASILS
ALBERTS/BLASTER/STABLER
ALBITES/BLASTIE/LIBATES
AMORETS   ANGELIC/ANGLICE
ANGERED/DERANGE/ENRAGED/GRANDEE/GRENADE
ASTHORE/EARSHOT/HAROSET
ATINGLE/ELATING/GELATIN/GENITAL

BALDIES/DISABLE   BRANSLE   BRANTLE
CANTLES/LANCETS   CARMINE
CENTERS/CENTRES/TENRECS CIGARET
CONSTER/CORNETS/CRESTON
COPIERS/PERSICO
DESMINE   DOLINES/INDOLES/SONDELI
DISCOER   DONSIER/INDORSE/ROSINED
DUNITES   ESPARTO/PROTEAS/SEAPORT
ETALONS   GALORES/GAOLERS
GENITOR   GRECIAN   HISTONE
HOGTIES
ISLEMAN/MALINES/MENIALS/SEMINAL
KINGLES   KINGLET   LESBIAN
LINOCUT   LINSEED
LISENTE/SETLINE/TENSILE
MAILERS/REALISM/REMAILS
MANTOES   MILTERS
MINERAL/RAILMEN
NAGARIS/SANGRIA/SARANGI
NAMASTE   NEUTRAL   NUTMEAL
OGREISH   ONSTAGE   ORGANIC
ORGEATS/STORAGE/TOERAGS
PALSIER/PARLIES   PAROLES/REPOSAL
PERIOST/REPOSIT/RIPOSTE/ROPIEST
PERSONA   PIOLETS/PISTOLE
SAPROBE   SEARATS   SOLERAS
STEDING/STINGED   SYRINGE   TELAMON
TENOURS/TONSURE
TEOPANS   TERTIAL   TONEARM

Notice how these lists are a mixture of the familiar, like **NEUTRAL**, the semi-familiar that you might not think of, like **NUTMEAL** and **PERSONA**, and the (almost certainly) unfamiliar, like **BRANSLE** and **BRANTLE** (variant spellings of an old French dance) and **SAPROBE** (an organism that lives in foul water). That's what makes these lists less alarming than they at first appear – you always have a head start with the words you know already.

You know what words can be made from **E E D I L N S** and **E G I N R S Y**; it's just a case of getting into your mind that when they appear on your rack you will change them into **LINSEED** and **SYRINGE**. In the same way, you will start to recognise the likes of **A C E I M N R** and **E H I N O S T**. Looking at the letters just sets off that little light-bulb in your head, and, with a bit of practice, it comes to you – **CARMINE** and **HISTONE**.

A FEW TEASERS

Try to find the seven-letter words from these combinations. They have been graded according to how easy or difficult you are likely to find them:

1 *Almost*-**RETAINS** *words:*

11-Plus:	**AEIMNRS**	**EINRSTW**
GCSE Level:	**AEGNRST**	**AENRSTV**
A Level:	**AEIMNRT**	**AINRSTT**
Degree:	**AEHINRT**	**EILNRST**
Doctorate:	**ABEINRT**	**AEHINST**

2 *Words with affixes:*

Dopy:	**ABEEELS**	**ADILSTY**
Dozy:	**AEIKLRT**	**EINQTUU**
Doughty:	**ABDENSU**	**DEEEKRY**
Deadly:	**ANOOPRS**	**EGILOST**

3 *Other useful words:*

Clown's car:	**ADEEGNR**	**AEILNOT**
Family car:	**ACGINOR**	**ADEEILM**
Sports car:	**ACEGIRT**	**ADEINOR**
Racing car:	**AEIMNOT**	**CILNOTU**

Answers are given at the back of the book.

9 Some eight-letter lists

You might not always be able to play a seven-letter word. In this chapter we look at some tips and lists to help you on your way to playing eight-letter words.

Unblocking a game

Every Scrabble game develops in a slightly different way. Sometimes there are lots of short words played parallel to each other, so the board ends up in an angry little knot of tiles clustered round the centre. If the words on the outside of this knot are 'blockers' (words which don't take any hooks either at the front or the end), it can get to a stage where it's very difficult to add anything at all.

A blocked opening to a game.

There isn't likely to be a bonus played with the next move on this first board. It's not impossible – there are eight-letter words ending in **U**, such as **HAUSFRAU**, **THANKYOU** and the rather unlikely **SUCURUJU**, or you might even come up with a nine-letter word using two on the board, like **CHLAMYDIA**, but, realistically, this won't happen.

A slight change to the opening makes all the difference.

On the second board (above), a seven-letter word can easily be played, using hooks such as **ITS**, **ITA**, **ABA**, **OBA**, **LAMA** or any two-letter word ending in **A**.

On the third board (on the next page), it looks like a bonus has been played already. It may not – the opening move might have been **QUAKE** or various other words (**WONDER**, **AKE**, **DE**, though none of these seems very likely to have produced the board as shown). Bonuses are certainly playable onto this board, but probably not a seven-letter word. You will have to use one of the free letters on the board (a '*floater*', in Scrabble jargon) to make an eight-letter word.

A board with a completely different kind of beginning.

Using floaters to make eight-letter words

There are plenty to choose from: **W**, **O**, **N**, **S**, **U**, **A** and, if you're feeling very clever, **Q**, are all in the middle of the board, and if you can combine any of them with the seven on your rack, you will be able to play a bonus. The **D** and the **R** are also possible to use, although they are restricted, and the **K** is just about possible, but hemmed in by other letters.

If you want to maximize the number of bonuses you play, you really need to be at home with eights as well as sevens. This chapter will put an army of high-probability eight-letter words at your disposal, all ready for you to slam down on the board for those longed-for 50 bonus points.

Learning about eight-letter words

Where to start? On the basis that you are still keeping those **RETAINS** letters from the last chapter, you could start with some eights containing those letters – the **RETAINS** + 1 list. Of course, a lot of them will be sevens from the **RETAIN** list with an **S** on the end: **DETRAINS**, **HAIRNETS**,

MINARETS, **TRANNIES** and many more. There seems little point in listing them – go back to the **RETAIN** list in the previous chapter and try to work them out for yourself.

However, there are a few more which aren't quite so simple. Here are a few **RETAINS** + 1 eights you might not know, or might not think of so easily.

A selection of **RETAINS** *+ 1 words*

A	ANTISERA	ARTESIAN	RATANIES	RESINATA	SEATRAIN
B	BANISTER	BARNIEST			
C	CANISTER	CARNIEST	CISTERNA	SCANTIER	
D	RANDIEST	STRAINED			
E	ARSENITE	RESINATE	STEARINE		
G	ASTRINGE	GANISTER	GANTRIES	RANGIEST	STEARING
I	RAINIEST				
K	NARKIEST				
O	ANOESTRI	ARSONITE	NOTARIES	ROSINATE	SENORITA
P	PANTRIES	PINASTER	PRISTANE		
R	RESTRAIN	STRAINER	TRANSIRE		
S	ARTINESS	SNARIEST			
T	STRAITEN				

Of course, you don't need to have **RETAINS** on your rack to play these; if you have six of **RETAINS**, and the seventh is 'floating' on the board, you effectively have the same thing and may well be able to play a **RETAINS** + 1 word.

Using floating letters to make an eight

It's also handy to know eights you can make from sets of seven common letters plus one other, when the seven letters don't make a bonus word. Few racks are more annoying than the ones with good letters you don't want to break up, but which don't make a bonus yet. With a rack like **A A E I N R T** (**RETAIN** + **A**), getting a good score can be difficult even playing five or six tiles. Just to play the **A** will probably get you a single-figure score, and while you might get the bonus next time, you might just pick the **Q** or the **X**, or another **A**.

But using a floating letter on the board you can solve the problem by conjuring up an eight. Here are some examples.

R E T A I N A +

B	RABATINE	
C	CARINATE	CRANIATE
D	DENTARIA	RAINDATE
G	AERATING	
M	ANIMATER	MARINATE
O	AERATION	
P	ANTIRAPE	
S	*See below*	
T	ATTAINER	REATTAIN
U	INAURATE	
W	ANTIWEAR	
Z	ATRAZINE	

It's a bit of an oddity that despite **RETAINA** not making a seven, there are a lot of eights you can make from **RETAINA** + **S**: you saw them in the **RETAINS** + 1 list:

ANTISERA	ARTESIAN	RATANIES
RESINATA	SEATRAIN	

Here are some more eights from good-looking but unproductive sevens (**A E E I N R S**, **A E I L O R S** and **D E E I N R T**).

AEEINRS+

C	CINEREAS	INCREASE	RESIANCE
D	ARSENIDE	DENARIES	DRAISENE	NEARSIDE
G	ANERGIES	GESNERIA	
H	INHEARSE		
K	SNEAKIER		
L	ALIENERS		
M	REMANIES		
N	ANSERINE		
P	NAPERIES		
R	REARISEN		
S	SENARIES		
T	ARENITES	ARSENITE	RESINATE	STEARINE
	TRAINEES		
U	UNEASIER		

AEILORS+

A	OLEARIAS		
C	CALORIES	CARIOLES	
D	DARIOLES	SOLIDARE	SOREDIAL
F	FORESAIL		
G	GASOLIER	GIRASOLE	SERAGLIO
H	AIRHOLES	SHOALIER	
M	MORALISE		
N	AILERONS	ALERIONS	ALIENORS
P	PELORIAS	POLARISE	

The list for **A E I L O R S** + above shows that any letter can be useful in the right circumstances; most people hate picking a **V** – perhaps club players more than most, because they know it's the only letter that doesn't make a two-letter word and so are instinctively scared of it. But if you're drawing an eighth letter to **A E I L O R S**, the best letter of all is **V**, forming four anagrams.

D E E I N R T +

A	DETAINER	RETAINED		
B	INTERBED			
D	DENDRITE			
K	TINKERED			
M	REMINTED			
N	INDENTER	INTENDER	INTERNED	
O	ORIENTED			
R	INTERRED	TRENDIER		
S	INSERTED	NERDIEST	RESIDENT	SINTERED
	TRENDIES			
T	RETINTED			
U	RETINUED	REUNITED		
V	INVERTED			
W	WINTERED			
X	DEXTRINE			

Eight-letter words using prefixes and suffixes

You can use prefixes and suffixes for eights just as much as for sevens – more so, as we have already noted, in the case of some of the four-letter affixes. So here's a selection of useful eights, with a selection of prefixes first.

Selection of eight-letter words listed by prefix

ANTI:	ANTIDOTE, ANTIFOAM, ANTIHERO, ANTIMERE, ANTIPORN
CON:	CONGLOBE, CONGREET, CONTANGO, CONTRAIL, CONURBAN
DE:	DEAERATE, DEBRUISE, DEGREASE, DERATTED, DESINING
DIS:	DISANNUL, DISCOURE, DISGAVEL, DISLEAVE, DISPLANT
EN:	ENCRADLE, ENHALOES, ENLARGEN, ENSAMPLE, ENSOULED
IN:	INDARTED, INFRUGAL, INNATIVE, INSEEMED, INSTABLE
MIS:	MISDREAD, MISGRAFT, MISLEARN, MISPLANT, MISTRACE
OUT:	OUTDRESS, OUTHOMER, OUTRANGE, OUTSMILE, OUTWEARY
OVER:	OVERDOER, OVERGILT, OVERMELT, OVERSALE, OVERWISE
PRE:	PREBLESS, PRECURSE, PRELIMIT, PRERINSE, PRETRIMS
PRO:	PROGRADE, PROMETAL, PROSTYLE, PROTONIC, PROVIRAL
SUB:	SUBAGENT, SUBCASTE, SUBGENUS, SUBLEASE, SUBTIDAL
UP:	UPBEARER, UPGATHER, UPGROWTH, UPSETTER, UPSTROKE

Eight-letter words starting with **RE–**

REASCENT	REINDUCT	REQUIGHT
REBODIES	REJACKET	REREWARD
RECANTER	REKINDLE	RESALUTE
REDECIDE	RELUMINE	RETARGET
REEMBODY	REMELTED	REUTTERS
REFRINGE	RENATURE	REVETTED
REGELATE	REOBTAIN	REWIDENS
REHARDEN	REPERUSE	REZONING

Eight-letter words starting with **UN–**

UNALLIED	UNJOINTS	UNREINED
UNBEREFT	UNKOSHER	UNSEARED
UNCHASTE	UNLETHAL	UNTAILED
UNDOCILE	UNMODISH	UNUNITED
UNELATED	UNNATIVE	UNVEILER
UNFEUDAL	UNORNATE	UNWINDER
UNGENIAL	UNPOETIC	UNYEANED
UNHAIRED	UNQUIETS	UNZIPPED
UNIDEAED		

Moving on to the suffixes, get your head round a few of these:

Selection of eight-letter words listed by suffix

ABLE:	ATONABLE, FINDABLE, LAPSABLE, NAMEABLE, SENDABLE
AGE:	BARONAGE, DIALLAGE, INTERAGE, PILOTAGE, STERNAGE
ANT:	COSECANT, GALIVANT, PENCHANT, RELEVANT, STAGNANT
ATE:	CORELATE, GEMINATE, LEVIRATE, OBTURATE, TITIVATE
ENT:	ERUMPENT, FECULENT, PLANGENT, PRURIENT, SCANDENT
IER:	BLUESIER, BRICKIER, CRUMMIER, FROGGIER, YOUTHIER
IEST:	DULLIEST, LAWNIEST, MOORIEST, RUGGIEST, WHITIEST
ISE/	CAPONISE/IZE, FABULISE/IZE, INFAMISE/IZE,
IZE:	PTYALISE/IZE, SOBERISE/IZE
ISH:	CAMELISH, FLIRTISH, POKERISH, SNEAKISH, TILEFISH
IST:	CANOEIST, CREOLIST, LUTENIST, PARODIST, TENORIST
LESS:	BATHLESS, CODELESS, HOOFLESS RIFTLESS, WARTLESS
LIKE:	CORDLIKE, EPICLIKE, MASTLIKE, SALTLIKE, VESTLIKE
LY:	BADGERLY, DATIVELY, GOLDENLY, PLAGUILY, TONISHLY
MAN/	CORPSMAN/MEN, HOTELMAN/MEN, LODESMAN/MEN,
MEN:	POINTMAN/MEN, SHIREMAN/MEN
NESS:	AWAYNESS, HERENESS, LONGNESS, NULLNESS, THATNESS
TION:	GELATION, LIBATION, NUDATION, PUNITION,
	SWAPTION

Using '6 + 2' lists

Coming back to the common letters, you need to know a good number of eights with six **RETAINS** letters and two others. Of course, we have seen a lot already – all the **RETAINS** + 1 and **RETAINA** + 1 words, to start with. However, it can do no harm to look at a few more. But setting out the **ATEBRIN** + 1 list, the **CINEAST** + 1 list and so on, would give a long and tedious series of lists, more likely to put readers off than engage their enthusiasm. It also has large numbers of duplicates – **ATEBRIN** + **C** = **CERTAIN** + **B**, and so on. (**BACTERIN**, in case you're wondering.)

Likewise, setting them out as '6 + 2' lists could give us some dauntingly long lists – there are 576 combinations of two letters (**AA**, **AB** and so on, through to **ZZ**) that could go with any six-letter set to form an eight. Obviously, no six letters go with all 576 or even get close, but there comes a time for most people when learning words to improve your game tips over from being interesting to just a chore. Some of you may feel you've passed that stage already.

But just to set out pages of words in no particular order, or even alphabetically, doesn't seem to be any improvement. So take a look at these '6 + 2' lists, which have been limited so as not to try the average reader's patience to exhaustion. Only about 30 two-letter combinations are given for any set of six letters. A maximum of two anagrams are given for any resulting eight-letter combination. And simple **S** endings on sevens we've already met have been excluded, as have eight-letter words we've seen already in other lists.

AC	CANARIES	CESARIAN
AG	ANGARIES	ARGINASE
BL	RINSABLE	
BM	MIRBANES	
BU	ANBURIES	URBANISE
CK	SKINCARE	
DL	ISLANDER	
DY	SYNEDRIA	
FO	FARINOSE	
FP	FIREPANS	PANFRIES
FS	FAIRNESS	SANSERIF
GK	SKEARING	
GY	RESAYING	SYNERGIA
HP	PARISHEN	SERAPHIN
IK	KAISERIN	
IN	SIRENIAN	
IY	YERSINIA	
KM	RAMEKINS	
KP	RANPIKES	
LV	RAVELINS	
LX	RELAXINS	
MU	ANEURISM	
MY	SEMINARY	
NO	RAISONNE	
NW	SWANNIER	
SU	ANURESIS	SENARIUS
SX	XERANSIS	
UZ	AZURINES	SUZERAIN

BC	BACTERIN	
CC	ACENTRIC	
CU	ANURETIC	
CV	NAVICERT	
DH	ANTHERID	
DP	DIPTERAN	
EH	ATHERINE	HERNIATE
EI	INERTIAE	
GM	EMIGRANT	REMATING
GV	GRIEVANT	VINTAGER
HP	PERIANTH	
HU	HAURIENT	
IL	INERTIAL	
LN	INTERNAL	
LO	ORIENTAL	RELATION
LP	TRAPLINE	TRIPLANE
MN	TRAINMEN	
MT	MARTINET	
MU	RUMINATE	
MW	WARIMENT	
MY	TYRAMINE	
OP	ATROPINE	
OR	ANTERIOR	
OT	TENTORIA	
PU	PAINTURE	
RW	INTERWAR	

AB	BASANITE	
AC	ESTANCIA	
AF	FANTASIE	
AH	ASTHENIA	
AT	ASTATINE	TANAISTE
BH	ABSINTHE	
CM	AMNESTIC	SEMANTIC
CV	CISTVAEN	VESICANT
DY	DESYATIN	
EV	NAIVETES	
FM	MANIFEST	
GU	SAUTEING	UNITAGES
GZ	TZIGANES	
IP	PIANISTE	
KU	UNAKITES	
KV	KISTVAEN	
MO	SOMNIATE	
OV	STOVAINE	
OX	SAXONITE	
PS	STEAPSIN	
PY	EPINASTY	
TV	TASTEVIN	
UV	SUIVANTE	

AH	HETAIRAS	
AT	ARIETTAS	ARISTATE
BO	SABOTIER	
CD	ACRIDEST	
CH	STICHERA	THERIACS
DI	IRISATED	
DK	STRAIKED	
DO	ASTEROID	
DP	DIPTERAS	TARSIPED
EE	EATERIES	
EP	PARIETES	PETARIES
EV	EVIRATES	
GT	STRIGATE	
HP	TRIPHASE	
HU	THESAURI	
HY	HYSTERIA	
IM	AIRTIMES	SERIATIM
IX	SEXTARII	
LO	SOTERIAL	
MU	MURIATES	SEMITAUR
MV	VITAMERS	
MW	WARTIMES	
MY	SYMITARE	
PW	WIRETAPS	
PY	ASPERITY	
SV	TRAVISES	
VY	VESTIARY	

AB	ANTBEARS	RATSBANE
AE	ARSENATE	SERENATA
AG	STARAGEN	TANAGERS
AL	ASTERNAL	
AM	SARMENTA	SEMANTRA
AO	ANOESTRA	
AV	TAVERNAS	TSAREVNA
BD	BANDSTER	BARTENDS
BG	BANGSTER	
CD	CANTREDS	
CE	CENTARES	SARCENET
DO	TORNADES	
EE	SERENATE	
EF	FENESTRA	
EJ	SERJEANT	
EO	EARSTONE	RESONATE
EU	SAUTERNE	
FO	SEAFRONT	
GO	RAGSTONE	STONERAG
GU	STRAUNGE	
OR	ANTRORSE	
OW	STONERAW	
PT	TRANSEPT	TRAPNEST

AD	INTRADAS	RADIANTS
AG	GRANITAS	
AI	INTARSIA	
AM	MARTIANS	TAMARINS
AP	ASPIRANT	PARTISAN
AZ	TZARINAS	
BD	ANTBIRDS	
BG	BRASTING	
BO	TABORINS	
CO	CANTORIS	
DK	STINKARD	
DO	DIATRONS	INTRADOS
DR	TRIDARNS	
DU	UNITARDS	
GK	KARTINGS	STARKING
GW	RINGTAWS	WRASTING
GY	STINGRAY	STRAYING
HO	TRAHISON	
KO	SKIATRON	
LO	TONSILAR	
OP	ATROPINS	
OS	ARSONIST	
OT	STRONTIA	
OU	RAINOUTS	SUTORIAN

CE	ENTERICS	SECRETIN	GV	STERVING	
DD	STRIDDEN		IL	NIRLIEST	NITRILES
DO	DRONIEST		IO	IRONIEST	
EE	ETERNISE	TEENSIER	IU	NEURITIS	
EI	ERINITES	NITERIES	KL	LINKSTER	STRINKLE
EO	ONERIEST	SEROTINE	LU	INSULTER	LUSTRINE
EX	INTERSEX		LY	TINSELRY	
EY	SERENITY		OR	INTRORSE	SNORTIER
FI	SNIFTIER		OY	TYROSINE	
GH	RIGHTENS		OZ	TRIZONES	
GL	LINGSTER	TRINGLES	TY	ENTRYIST	
GT	GITTERNS		UV	UNRIVETS	VENTURIS

Some purists will be unhappy that I have chosen to give only selections of each of these lists, but this is not a book of word lists only. I have tried to achieve a balance between the lists and the rest of the book, and did not want to overwhelm newcomers to this side of the game with vast unlearnable numbers of new words. For those who want to see full lists from which these are a selection, other books and sources are available.

I have tried to include words which are likely to appear on your rack, and which are also memorable in some way. Perhaps you have been struck by the dependable rhythm of **BEELIKE**, **FATLIKE**, **NETLIKE**, **RATLIKE**, **TINLIKE**, the unexpected poetry of **GASOLIER**, **GIRASOLE**, **SERAGLIO** or the sheer serendipitousness of discovering that the anagram of **FAIRNESS** is **SANSERIF**. Playing words like **KINGLET**, **STONERAW** and **ERUMPENT** will bring a wow factor to your game that everyday words will never match.

> *Scrabble tip* – *Memorable anagrams are fun and a great way of getting words to stick. Here are some good eight-letter anagrams:*
>
> **LAMPPOST / PALMTOPS**
> **HANDOUTS / THOUSAND**
> **LAKELETS / SKELETAL**
> **EPITAPHS / HAPPIEST**
> **LICKSPIT / LIPSTICK**
> **STEWPANS / WASPNEST**
>
> *But my favourite eight-letter anagram has to be the two words from the letters* **ABEGMNOY**. *They are both common 5–3 compound words. Can you get them?*
>
> *Of course…* **BOGEYMAN** *and* **MONEYBAG**.

So do try and learn as many of these words as you can, even if only a few at a time. Your three-letter words, your clever little parallel plays, and your sticking down **EX** for 36 points are all very well, but it is the bonuses that will lift your game to a new level. Learn them, use them, treasure them.

SOME GREAT PUZZLES TO TRY

Find as many eight-letter words as you can on these boards with the racks shown.

1.
Your rack: **A E I N R S T**

2.
Your rack: **A E E I N R S**

3.
Your rack: **A D E L N T U**

4.
Your rack: **A C E I N R T**

10 Help with unusual letter combinations

A challenge that every Scrabble player faces at some point in almost every game is dealing with an unpromising combination of letters on their rack. Having too many of the same letter, too many vowels or too many consonants can put you in a situation where it is very difficult to come up with a viable word, let alone a high-scoring one.

This section contains various lists that may prove useful in dealing with an awkward combination of tiles, because they consist of words with unusual letter combinations.

Words from World English

One method of dealing with the awkward tile combinations that inevitably appear on your rack at some point in a game is to memorize a wide selection of words outside the core vocabulary of English. As the most widely spoken language in the world, English is rich in loan-words from other languages, and the versatility of the Roman alphabet and of English pronunciation means that these words tend to be assimilated without much corruption of their original sound. This means that there are many words in English that use 'foreign' letter combinations, which are ideal for Scrabble players. The following lists contain words from Australia, Canada, New Zealand and South Africa, as well as words from the main languages of the Indian Subcontinent – Hindi and Urdu – which have entered British English.

Australian words

Australian English is distinguished not only by the numerous Aboriginal terms for Australia's flora and fauna, but also by a great many shortened forms of commonplace English words. The Australian propensity to slang and short informal words is extremely useful to Scrabble players, especially as many of these words end in **O**, one of the most common tiles in the game. If you spot an **O** on the board when you have a difficult set of letters on your rack, there's a good chance that you'll be able to form an informal Aussie word. Native Australian words provide a range of unusual letter combinations, as well as a tendency to include double **O**s – ideal for rack balancing. Double **R**s are also common in Australian English, as are **K**s and **Y**s, so it's well worth acquiring some Antipodean vocabulary.

ADJIGO	yam plant	**BODGIE**	unruly or uncouth man
ALF	an uncultivated Australian	**BOGAN**	fool
ARVO	afternoon	**BOOBOOK**	small spotted brown owl
ASPRO	associate professor		
BARRO	embarrassing	**BOOFY**	strong but stupid
BAUERA	small evergreen shrub	**BOONG**	*offensive word* for a Black person
BEAUT	outstanding person or thing	**BOOSHIT**	very good
BELAH	casuarina tree	**BORA**	native Australian coming-of-age ceremony
BERKO	berserk		
BIFFO	fighting or aggressive behaviour	**BORAK**	rubbish or nonsense
BILBY	burrowing marsupial	**BRASCO**	lavatory
BIZZO	empty and irrelevant talk	**BROLGA**	large grey crane with red-and-green head
BOAB	baobab tree	**BRUMBY**	wild horse

BUNYA	tall dome-shaped coniferous tree	**DINKUM**	genuine or right
BUNYIP	legendary monster	**DOCO**	documentary
CADAGI	tropical eucalyptus tree	**DONGA**	steep-sided gully
		DORBA	stupid, inept or clumsy person
CARBY	carburettor	**DRACK**	unattractive
CHEWIE	chewing gum	**DRONGO**	slow-witted person
CHIACK	tease or banter	**DROOB**	pathetic person
CHOCO	conscript or militiaman	**DUBBO**	stupid
		DUGITE	venomous snake
CHOOK	hen or chicken	**DURRY**	cigarette
CHOOM	Englishman	**EARBASH**	talk incessantly
COMMO	communist	**EMU**	large flightless bird
COMPO	compensation	**EUMUNG**	type of acacia
CORREA	evergreen shrub	**EVO**	evening
COUCAL	long-legged bird	**EXO**	excellent
COUGAN	rowdy person	**FASTIE**	deceitful act
CRONK	unfit or unsound	**FESTY**	dirty or smelly
CROOL	spoil	**FIBRO**	house built of fibro-cement
CROWEA	pink-flowered shrub		
DACK	forcibly remove someone's trousers	**FIGJAM**	very conceited person
DADAH	illegal drugs	**FIZGIG**	frivolous or flirtatious girl
DAGGY	untidy or dishevelled		
		FOULIE	bad mood
DASYURE	small carnivorous marsupial	**FRIB**	short heavy-conditioned piece of wool
DELO	delegate		
DERRO	vagrant	**FUNDIE**	fundamentalist Christian
DINGO	wild dog		

FURPHY	rumour or fictitious story	**JUMBUCK**	sheep
GALAH	grey-and-pink cockatoo	**KARRI**	type of eucalyptus tree
		KOALA	slow-moving arboreal marsupial
GARBO	dustman	**KOORI**	native Australian
GEEBUNG	tree with edible but tasteless fruit	**KYBO**	temporary lavatory
		KYLIE	boomerang that is flat on one side and convex on the other
GIDGEE	small acacia tree that sometimes emits an unpleasant smell		
GILGAI	natural water hole	**LOPPY**	man employed to do maintenance work on a ranch
GING	child's catapult		
GNOW	ground-dwelling bird	**LOWAN**	ground-dwelling bird
GOANNA	monitor lizard	**LUBRA**	Aboriginal woman
GOOG	egg	**MALLEE**	low shrubby eucalyptus tree
GOOLIE	stone or pebble		
GUNYAH	bush hut or shelter	**MARRI**	type of eucalyptus
GYMPIE	tall tree with stinging hairs on its leaves	**MIDDY**	middle-sized glass of beer
HAKEA	type of shrub or tree	**MILKO**	milkman
HOSTIE	air hostess	**MOLOCH**	spiny lizard
HOVEA	plant with purple flowers	**MOPOKE**	small spotted owl
		MOZ	hoodoo or hex
HUTCHIE	groundsheet draped over an upright stick as a temporary shelter	**MUGGA**	eucalyptus tree with pink flowers and dark bark
JARRAH	type of eucalyptus tree	**MULGA**	acacia shrub
		MULLOCK	waste material from a mine
JEFF	downsize or close down an organization	**MURREE**	native Australian

MURRI	native Australian		**POONCE**	male homosexual
MUSO	musician		**POSSIE**	position
MYALL	native Australian living independently of society		**PRELOVED**	second-hand
			QUOKKA	small wallaby
			QUOLL	native cat
MYXO	myxomatosis		**RAZOO**	imaginary coin
NANA	head		**REFFO**	*offensive term* for a European refugee after World War Two
NARDOO	cloverlike fern			
NEDDY	horse			
NOAH	shark		**REGO**	registration of a motor vehicle
NONG	stupid or incompetent person			
			RESTO	restored antique, vintage car, etc
NORK	female breast			
NUDDY	in the nude		**ROO**	kangaroo
NUMBAT	small marsupial with long snout		**ROUGHIE**	something unfair, especially a trick
OCKER	uncultivated or boorish Australian		**SANGER**	sandwich
			SANGO	sandwich
PIKER	wild bullock		**SCOZZA**	rowdy person
PINDAN	desert region of Western Australia		**SCUNGY**	miserable, sordid or dirty
PITURI	shrub with narcotic leaves		**SHARPIE**	member of a teenage group with short hair and distinctive clothes
PLONKO	alcoholic, especially one who drinks wine			
PLURRY	*euphemism* for bloody		**SHERANG**	boss
PODDY	handfed calf or lamb		**SHYPOO**	liquor of poor quality
POKIE	poker machine			
POON	stupid or ineffectual person		**SITELLA**	small black-and-white bird

SKEG	rear fin on the underside of a surfboard		**VEGO**	vegetarian
			VIGORO	women's game similar to cricket
SKITE	boast		**WADDY**	heavy wooden club used by native Australians
SMOKO	cigarette break			
SMOODGE	smooch			
SPAG	*offensive term* for an Italian		**WAGGA**	blanket made of sacks stitched together
SPRUIK	speak in public		**WALLABY**	marsupial resembling a small kangaroo
SWAGGIE	vagrant worker			
SWAGMAN	vagrant worker		**WANDOO**	eucalyptus tree with white bark
SWY	gambling game			
TONK	effeminate man		**WARATAH**	shrub with dark green leaves and crimson flowers
TOOSHIE	angry or upset			
TRIELLA	three horse races nominated for a bet			
			WARB	dirty or insignificant person
TROPPO	mentally affected by a tropical climate			
			WHARFIE	wharf labourer
TRUCKIE	truck driver		**WIDGIE**	female bodgie
TRUGO	game similar to croquet		**WILGA**	small drought-resistant tree
TUAN	flying phalanger		**WIRILDA**	acacia tree with edible seeds
TUART	type of eucalyptus tree			
			WIRRAH	saltwater fish with bright blue spots
UMPIE	umpire			
UNCO	awkward or clumsy		**WOF**	fool or idiot
UPTA	of poor quality		**WOMBAT**	burrowing marsupial
UPTER	of poor quality		**WOOMERA**	spear-throwing stick
UTE	utility		**WURLEY**	Aboriginal hut
VAG	vagrant		**YABBER**	talk or jabber

YABBY	small freshwater crayfish	**YUCKO**	disgusting
YACCA	grass tree	**YUMMO**	delicious
YACKA	grass tree	**ZAMBUCK**	St John Ambulance attendant
YARRAN	small hardy tree	**ZIFF**	beard
YATE	small eucalyptus tree		
YIKE	argument, squabble or fight		

Canadian words

Canadian English combines a broad range of British and US terms with words derived from Inuit, as well as from other Native American languages such as Algonquin. Canadian English incorporates many Canadian French words from Québec, and there are also a number of recently coined Canadian terms. Inuit words can be helpful to Scrabble players because they tend to be quite vowel-heavy. **K** occurs frequently in Inuit terms, and sometimes appears twice. Such words require a blank tile for the second **K** if they are to be played during a game.

AGLOO	breathing hole made in ice by a seal	**BABICHE**	thongs or lacings of rawhide
AGLU	breathing hole made in ice by a seal	**BARACHOIS**	shallow lagoon formed by a sand bar
AMAUT	hood on an Inuit woman's parka for carrying a child	**BATEAU**	light flat-bottomed boat
AMOWT	hood on an Inuit woman's parka for carrying a child	**BEIGNET**	deep-fried pastry
		BOGAN	sluggish side stream
ATIGI	Inuit parka	**BREWIS**	Newfoundland cod stew

BUTTE	isolated steep-sided flat-topped hill	**KLOOCH**	North American Indian woman
CABOOSE	mobile bunkhouse used by lumbermen	**KLOOTCH**	North American Indian woman
CANOLA	cooking oil extracted from a variety of Canadian rapeseed	**KUDLIK**	Inuit soapstone seal-oil lamp
		LOGAN	backwater
CAYUSE	small Native American pony used by cowboys	**LOONIE**	Canadian dollar coin with loon bird on one face
COULEE	dry stream valley		
CUSK	gadoid food fish	**MUCKAMUCK** food	
DEKE	act or instance of feinting in ice hockey	**MUKTUK**	beluga skin used as food
GROWLER	small iceberg that has broken off from a larger iceberg or glacier	**NANOOK**	polar bear
		PARFLECHE dried rawhide	
		PARKADE	building used as a car park
HONKER	Canada goose	**PARKETTE**	small public park
HOSER	unsophisticated rural person	**PLEW**	beaver skin used as standard unit in fur trading
ICEWINE	dessert wine made from frozen grapes		
		POGEY	financial relief for the unemployed
JIGGER	device used when setting a gill net beneath ice	**POGY**	financial relief for the unemployed
JOUAL	nonstandard Canadian French dialect	**POKELOGAN** backwater	
		POUTINE	chipped potatoes topped with curd cheese and tomato sauce
KAMIK	Inuit boot made of caribou hide or sealskin		

PUNG	horse-drawn sleigh		**TILLICUM**	friend
REDEYE	drink incorporating beer and tomato juice		**TOONIE**	Canadian two-dollar coin
RUBABOO	soup made by boiling pemmican		**TULLIBEE**	whitefish found in the Great Lakes
RUBBY	rubbing alcohol mixed with cheap wine for drinking		**TUPEK**	Inuit tent of animal skins
SKOOKUM	strong or brave		**TUPIK**	Inuit tent of animal skins
SNYE	side channel of a river		**TWONIE**	Canadian two-dollar coin
SPLAKE	hybrid trout bred by Canadian zoologists		**WAWA**	speech or language
SWILER	seal hunter		**WENDIGO**	evil spirit or cannibal

Hindi words

After Chinese, Hindi, the dominant language of India, is the most widely spoken language in the world. Many Hindi words entered British English during the Raj, and some have become everyday terms – **BUNGALOW** and **PUNDIT**, for example. Others are less common, but are useful to Scrabble players because they provide unusual letter combinations and thus solutions to difficult racks. Combinations such as **BH**, **DH** and **KH** are common in Hindi-derived words, and the preponderance of **A**s, **I**s and **U**s can be very helpful in trying to balance a vowel-heavy rack. Above all, Hindi words are useful because they are quite unusual, and so provide a range of options for Scrabble players that aren't immediately obvious – front-hooking onto **HANG** with a **B**, for example, or end-hooking onto **PUNK** with an **A**. Committing some Hindi-derived words to memory will help to keep your opponents on their toes.

AKHARA	gymnasium	**BOBBERY**	mixed pack of
ALAP	vocal music without		hunting dogs
	words	**BUND**	embankment
AMBARY	tropical plant	**CHAI**	tea, especially with
ANKUS	elephant goad		added spices
ANNA	old copper coin	**CHAMPAC**	tree with fragrant
ARTI	Hindu ritual		yellow flowers
AYAH	maidservant or	**CHAPATI**	flat coarse unleavened
	nursemaid		bread
BABU	Mr	**CHAPPAL**	sandal
BAEL	spiny tree	**CHARAS**	hashish
BAHADUR	title for distinguished	**CHARKHA**	spinning wheel
	Indians during the Raj	**CHEETAH**	large swift feline
BANDH	general strike		mammal
BANYAN	tree with aerial roots	**CHETAH**	large swift feline
BHAJI	deep-fried vegetable		mammal
	savoury	**CHELA**	disciple of a religious
BHANG	psychoactive drug		teacher
	made of hemp	**CHICHI**	person of mixed
BHANGRA	music combining		British and Indian
	traditional Punjabi		descent
	music with Western	**CHILLUM**	pipe for smoking
	pop		cannabis
BHAVAN	large house or	**CHINTZ**	printed cotton with
	building		glazed finish
BHEESTY	water-carrier	**CHITAL**	large, spotted deer
BHINDI	okra used in cooking	**CHOKEY**	prison
BHISHTI	water-carrier	**CHOLI**	short-sleeved bodice
BINDI	decorative dot in	**CHOWK**	marketplace
	middle of forehead	**CHUDDAR**	large shawl or veil

CHUDDIES	underpants	**DHAL**	curry made from
CHUKAR	Indian partridge		lentils
CHUKKA	period of play in polo	**DHARNA**	method of obtaining
CHUTNEY	Indian pickle		justice by fasting
COOLIE	cheaply hired	**DHOBI**	washerman
	unskilled labourer	**DHOTI**	loincloth
COOLY	cheaply hired	**DUPATTA**	scarf
	unskilled labourer	**DURBAR**	court of an Indian
COWAGE	tropical climbing		ruler
	plant with stinging	**DURRIE**	cotton carpet
	pods	**DURZI**	Indian tailor
COWHAGE	tropical climbing	**GANJA**	potent form of
	plant with stinging		cannabis
	pods	**GAUR**	large wild cow
CRORE	ten million	**GARIAL**	fish-eating
CUSHY	comfortable		crocodilian with long
DACOIT	a member of a gang		slender snout
	of armed robbers	**GAVIAL**	fish-eating
DACOITY	robbery by an armed		crocodilian with long
	gang		slender snout
DAK	system of mail delivery	**GHARIAL**	fish-eating
DAL	split grain		crocodilian with long
DATURA	plant with trumpet-		slender snout
	shaped flowers	**GHARRI**	horse-drawn vehicle
DEKKO	look or glance		for hire
DEODAR	Himalayan cedar	**GHARRY**	horse-drawn vehicle
DEWAN	chief minister of an		for hire
	Indian princedom	**GHAT**	stairs or passage
DHAK	tropical tree with red		leading down to a
	flowers		river

GHEE	clarified butter
GHERAO	industrial action in which workers imprison their employers
GINGILI	oil obtained from sesame seeds
GORAL	small goat antelope
GUAR	plant that produces gum
GUNNY	coarse fabric used for sacks
GURU	Hindu or Sikh religious teacher
HARTAL	act of closing shop or stopping work as a political protest
HOWDAH	seat for riding on an elephant's back
JAGGERY	coarse brown sugar
JAI	victory
KHADDAR	cotton cloth
KHEDA	enclosure for captured elephants
KHEDAH	enclosure for captured elephants
KHEDDAH	enclosure for captured elephants
KOEL	parasitic cuckoo
KOS	Indian unit of distance
KRAIT	brightly coloured venomous snake
KUKRI	Gurkha knife
KULFI	Indian dessert
KURTA	long loose garment like a shirt without a collar
LAC	resinous substance secreted by insects
LAKH	100,000
LANGUR	arboreal monkey
LASSI	yoghurt drink
LATHI	long heavy stick used as a weapon
LUNGI	long piece of cloth worn as loincloth or turban
MACHAN	platform used in tiger hunting
MAHOUT	elephant driver
MAHSEER	large freshwater fish
MANDI	big market
MANDIR	Hindu or Jain temple
MAUND	unit of weight
MEHNDI	practice of painting designs on the hands and feet using henna
MELA	cultural or religious festival
MOHUR	old gold coin

MONAL	Asian pheasant	**PURDA**	custom of keeping women secluded
MORCHA	hostile demonstration against the government	**PURDAH**	custom of keeping women secluded
MRIDANG	drum used in Indian music	**PURI**	unleavened flaky bread
MYNAH	tropical starling	**PUTTEE**	strip of cloth wound around the leg
NAUCH	intricate Indian dance	**RAGGEE**	cereal grass
NAUTCH	intricate Indian dance	**RAGI**	cereal grass
NAWAB	Muslim prince in India	**RAITA**	yoghurt-and-vegetable dish served with curry
NEEM	large tree		
NILGAI	large Indian antelope		
NULLAH	stream or drain	**RAJ**	government
NUMDAH	coarse felt	**RAJAH**	ruler or landlord
OONT	camel	**RAMTIL**	African plant grown in India
PACHISI	game resembling backgammon	**RANEE**	queen or princess
PAISA	one hundredth of a rupee	**RANI**	queen or princess
PAKORA	dish of deep-fried chicken or vegetables	**RATHA**	four-wheeled carriage drawn by horses or bullocks
PANEER	soft white cheese	**ROTI**	type of unleavened bread
PARATHA	flat unleavened bread		
PEEPUL	tree similar to the banyan	**RUPEE**	standard monetary unit of India
PUNKA	fan made of palm leaves	**RUPIAH**	standard monetary unit of Indonesia
PUNKAH	fan made of palm leaves	**RYOT**	peasant or tenant farmer

SAMBAR	deer with three-tined antlers	**TONGA**	light two-wheeled vehicle
SAMITI	political association	**TOPEE**	pith helmet
SAMOSA	triangular pastry containing spiced vegetables or meat	**TOPI**	pith helmet
		URD	bean plant
		VAHANA	vehicle in Indian myth
SARANGI	stringed instrument played with a bow	**VANDA**	type of orchid
SARDAR	Sikh title	**VINA**	stringed musical instrument
SARI	traditional dress of Indian women	**WALLAH**	person in charge of a specific thing
SAROD	Indian stringed instrument	**ZENANA**	part of a house reserved for women and girls
SWAMI	title for a Hindu saint or religious teacher		
TABLA	pair of drums whose pitches can be varied	**ZILA**	administrative district in India
THALI	meal consisting of several small dishes	**ZILLA**	administrative district in India
TIL	sesame	**ZILLAH**	administrative district in India
TOLA	unit of weight		

New Zealand words

While New Zealand and Australian English have many words in common, the Kiwi lexicon is greatly enriched by New Zealand's Maori heritage. Maori-derived words are a marvellous resource for the Scrabble player, providing a wealth of unusual vowel combinations, and frequently using consonants that are rarer in European words, such as **K**, **W** and **H**. Maori words are especially good for balancing vowel-heavy racks, as many words use several **A**s, **U**s or **I**s – sometimes with three vowels in a row. Relatively high-scoring consonants are also very common, especially **K** and **H**. Unfortunately, there is only one **K** in Scrabble, so many Maori words with two **K**s are less useful than they might initially appear. Don't forget blank tiles, however: if you have a blank, a **K** and a couple of vowels on your rack, there's a good chance that you can find a New Zealand word to play profitably. There are also some unusual words that have entered the vocabulary of New Zealanders from European or Asian languages.

ATUA	spirit or demon		**JANOLA**	household bleach
BOOHAI	thoroughly lost		**KAHAWAI**	large fish
COOTIE	body louse		**KAI**	food
GOORIE	mongrel dog		**KAIK**	village
GRAUNCH	crush or destroy		**KAINGA**	village
HAKA	war dance		**KAKA**	long-billed parrot
HANGI	open-air cooking pit		**KAKAPO**	ground-dwelling
HAPU	subtribe			parrot
HAPUKA	large fish		**KARAKIA**	prayer
HAPUKU	large fish		**KARANGA**	call or chant of
HEITIKI	neck ornament			welcome
HIKOI	protest march		**KATIPO**	small venomous
HOKONUI	illicit whisky			spider
HONGI	nose-touching		**KAUPAPA**	strategy, policy or
	greeting			cause
HUHU	hairy beetle		**KAURI**	coniferous tree
HUI	conference or meeting		**KAWA**	protocol or etiquette
HUIA	extinct New Zealand		**KIEKIE**	climbing bush plant
	bird		**KIWI**	flightless bird with
JAFA	*offensive term* for			long beak and no tail
	someone from		**KOHA**	gift or donation
	Auckland		**KOKAKO**	long-tailed crow

KONEKE	farm vehicle	**PIUPIU**	leaf skirt
KORU	curved pattern	**POI**	ball of woven flax
KOWHAI	small tree	**PONGA**	tall tree fern
KUIA	female elder	**PORAE**	edible sea fish
KURI	mongrel dog	**PORANGI**	crazy
KUTU	body louse	**PORINA**	moth larva
MANUKA	myrtaceous tree	**POTAE**	hat
MATAI	evergreen tree	**POWHIRI**	welcoming ceremony
MIHI	ceremonial greeting	**PUGGY**	sticky
MOA	extinct large flightless	**PUHA**	sow thistle
	bird	**PUKEKO**	wading bird
MOKI	edible sea fish	**PURIRI**	forest tree
MOKO	Maori tattoo or	**RAHUI**	Maori prohibition
	tattoo pattern	**RATA**	myrtaceous forest tree
MOOLOO	person from Waikato	**RAUPATU**	seizure of land
MOPOKE	small spotted owl	**RAURIKI**	sow thistle
MUNGA	army canteen	**SHEEPO**	person who brings
NGAIO	small tree		sheep to the catching
NGATI	tribe or clan		pen for shearing
NIKAU	palm tree	**TAIAHA**	ceremonial fighting
PAKAHI	acid soil or land		staff
PAKAPOO	Chinese lottery	**TAIHOA**	hold on!
PAKOKO	small freshwater fish	**TAKAHE**	rare flightless bird
PAUA	edible abalone	**TANGI**	Maori funeral
PERFING	early retirement from		ceremony
	the police force with	**TANIWHA**	legendary monster
	financial	**TAONGA**	treasure
	compensation	**TAPU**	sacred or forbidden
PIKAU	rucksack	**TARSEAL**	bitumen surface of
PIPI	shellfish		a road

TAUIWI	non-Maori people of New Zealand		**WEKA**	flightless bird
			WERO	warrior's challenge
TIKANGA	Maori customs		**WETA**	long-legged wingless insect
TOETOE	type of tall grass			
TOITOI	type of tall grass		**WHANAU**	family
TWINK	white correction fluid		**WHENAU**	native land
WAKA	Maori canoe			

South African words

South African English includes words from Nguni languages such as Xhosa and Zulu, as well as Afrikaans, amongst other languages. For Scrabble players, South African English offers a host of useful words for balancing vowel-heavy racks. Many Afrikaans-derived words contain a double **A**, while Nguni words often contain two or three **A**s. It's a good idea, therefore, to have some South African words up your sleeve for when you find yourself with two or more **A**s on your rack. There are also a lot of **K** words in South African English. As **K** can be an awkward letter to use effectively, these can come in very handy, as can the Afrikaans-derived words containing **V**, which are most helpful in trying to use a difficult tile.

AMADODA	grown men		**DAGGA**	marijuana
AMANDLA	political slogan calling for power to the Black population		**DWAAL**	state of befuddlement
			GEELBEK	yellow-jawed fish
			HAMBA	go away
BAAS	boss		**JA**	yes
BABALAS	drunk or hung over		**JAAP**	simpleton
BAKKIE	small truck		**JEREPIGO**	heavy desert wine
BRAAI	grill or roast meat		**JONG**	friend
BRAAIVLEIS	barbecue		**KAAL**	naked
BUNDU	wild, remote region		**KEREL**	chap or fellow

KRAAL	stockaded village	**ROOIKAT**	lynx
KWAITO	type of pop music	**SCAMTO**	argot of urban South
LEGUAAN	large monitor lizard		African Blacks
MEERKAT	sociable mongoose	**SKOLLY**	hooligan
MENEER	Mr or Sir	**SNOEK**	edible marine fish
MEVROU	Mrs or Madam	**SPEK**	bacon, fat or fatty
MOOI	pleasing		pork
MUTI	herbal medicine	**STEEN**	variety of white
NAARTJIE	tangerine		grape
NEK	mountain pass	**STOKVEL**	savings pool or
NKOSI	master or chief		syndicate
OKE	man	**VLEI**	area of marshy
OOM	title of respect		ground
OUBAAS	person senior in	**VOEMA**	vigour or energy
	rank or years	**VOETSEK**	expression of
PADKOS	snacks for a long		dismissal or rejection
	journey	**VROU**	woman or wife
PLAAS	farm	**YEBO**	yes

Urdu words

Urdu, the official language of Pakistan and one of the official languages
of India, is closely related to Hindi. Urdu, however, contains many more
words derived from Arabic and Persian, and also uses a different system of
writing from Hindi, lending a different character to the words that have
entered English. Many Urdu culinary terms will be familiar to British
Scrabble players from Indian restaurants, while most Anglo-Indian military
vocabulary also derives from Urdu rather than Hindi. As with Hindi, the
variant spellings of many Urdu words provide opportunities for Scrabble
players, as does the frequency of the letter **K**.

BAGH	garden	**KEBAB**	dish of meat, onions, etc, grilled on skewers
BALTI	spicy Indian dish stewed until most liquid has evaporated	**KHAKI**	dull yellowish-brown colour
BASTI	slum	**KHARIF**	crop harvested at beginning of winter
BEGUM	woman of high rank		
BIRIANI	Indian dish of highly flavoured rice mixed with meat or fish	**KHAYAL**	kind of Indian classical vocal music
BIRYANI	Indian dish of highly flavoured rice mixed with meat or fish	**KINCOB**	fine silk fabric embroidered with gold or silver threads
BUSTEE	slum	**KOFTA**	Indian dish of seasoned minced meat shaped into balls
BUSTI	slum		
CHARPAI	bedstead of woven webbing on a wooden frame	**KOFTGAR**	person skilled in inlaying steel with gold
CHARPOY	bedstead of woven webbing on a wooden frame	**KOFTGARI**	art of inlaying steel with gold
DAROGHA	manager	**KORMA**	Indian dish of meat or vegetables braised with yoghurt or cream
DHANSAK	Indian dish of meat or vegetables braised with lentils		
INQILAB	revolution	**LASCAR**	sailor from the East Indies
IZZAT	honour or prestige		
JACONET	light cotton fabric	**MAIDAN**	open space used for meetings and sports
JEMADAR	officer in the Indian police		
KAMEEZ	long tunic	**MASALA**	mixed spices ground into a paste

MOOLVI	Muslim doctor of the law	**SHIKAREE**	hunter
MOOLVIE	Muslim doctor of the law	**SHIKARI**	hunter
		SICE	servant who looks after horses
MURDABAD	down with; death to	**SUBADAH**	chief native office in a company of sepoys
MUSTH	frenzied sexual excitement in male elephants	**SUBADAR**	chief native office in a company of sepoys
NUMDAH	coarse felt	**SUBAH**	chief native office in a company of sepoys
QORMA	Indian dish of meat or vegetables braised with yoghurt or cream	**SYCE**	servant who looks after horses
RABI	crop harvested at the end of winter	**TAHSIL**	administrative division
		TALOOKA	subdivision of a district
SAHIB	title placed after a man's name	**TALUK**	subdivision of a district
SAICE	servant who looks after horses	**TALUKA**	subdivision of a district
SARPANCH	head of a village council	**TAMASHA**	show or entertainment
SEPOY	Indian soldier in the service of the British	**TANDOORI**	method of cooking on a spit in a clay oven
SHALWAR	loose-fitting trousers		
SHIKAR	hunting		

11 Ending the game

So, you've learned your twos, most of your threes, and some useful fours. You've got maximum value from whatever high-value tiles you picked up, you've used your new-found confidence in finding sevens and eights, especially with an **S** or a blank, to make a couple of bonus words, and you have increased your vocabulary from the great variety of world English. The only problem is, your opponent, being one of those annoying people, has done the exact same thing.

Final pointers

You are now approaching the end of the game, and the scores are close. Whether it's about 200 each or 400 each doesn't matter. Your score as such has become irrelevant. You want to win the game.

It won't always happen this way. In a game between two evenly matched players, one can get all the luck, or just that little bit when it matters, and run out the winner by 200 or 300 points. A weaker player can often beat a stronger one over one game. That's why tournament players always like to settle important tournaments over a number of matches – not necessarily all against the same player, but against a number of players of similar standard. Then the cream tends to rise to the top. A one-off win proves nothing.

But let's assume you are playing a game now and, with few or no tiles left in the bag, the scores are close. How do you find that vital edge?

Essentially, what you are now trying to do is not just maximize your own score but also minimize your opponent's. And to do that, you need to know what letters your opponent has got, or know as nearly as is possible. You do this by tile-tracking.

The need for tile-tracking

Back at the beginning of the book we talked about counting up whether more **A**s or **I**s had been played. If given a choice, you could then play whichever there were more of left in the bag, making you less likely to be left with an awkward duplicate. *Tile-tracking* is an extension of this tactic, and relies on the fact that you know exactly how many of each letter were in the bag at the start of the game. You also know what's been played – it's all there in front of you. And you know what's on your rack. It's simple arithmetic to work out what's left – and that must be what is on your opponent's rack or still in the bag.

I'll repeat again what I said about the **A**s and **I**s. A card player – such as in bridge or poker – will always try to remember what cards have been turned over and are therefore not in the hands of the other players or still in the pack to be dealt. It's an accepted – indeed essential – part of good play. So it is in Scrabble, but with the advantage that all that tough memory work is eliminated. Everything that's been played in Scrabble is face up. It's hard enough remembering over 200,000 allowable words without remembering whether or not somebody played the second **F** twenty minutes ago. Fortunately you don't have to. Just look at the board.

Using a tile-tracking sheet

Even better, look at your tile-tracking sheet. A tile-tracking sheet is a pre-prepared list or grid of letters, which you cross off as each tile is played. At the end of the game, what you haven't crossed off is what's still to come.

Different people use different types of tracking sheet. Some list the letters **A–Z**, plus blank, down one side of the sheet, and mark a tick against each as it is played (see Tile-Tracking Sheet 1 opposite). Towards the end of the game, if there are only eight ticks against the letter **A**, you know there is one to come, as there are nine in the set.

Some make the relevant number of ticks against each letter at the start of the game and then cross them off, so the number of ticks left is the number of that letter still to be played (see Tile-Tracking Sheet 2 on the next page). Some write out all hundred letters and cross them through as they are played (see Tile-Tracking Sheet 3 on the next page).

Three different styles of tile-tracking sheet, each shown part way through a game are shown.

Tile-Tracking Sheet 1

A	✓✓✓✓✓	O	✓✓✓✓✓
B	✓	P	✓✓
C	✓✓	Q	✓
D	✓✓✓	R	✓✓✓✓
E	✓✓✓✓✓✓✓	S	✓✓
F	✓	T	✓✓✓✓✓
G	✓	U	✓✓✓
H	✓✓	V	
I	✓✓✓✓	W	✓✓
J	✓	X	✓
K		Y	✓
L	✓✓✓	Z	✓
M	✓	?	✓
N	✓✓✓✓		

Tile-Tracking Sheet 2

A ~~A A A A~~ ✓ ✓ ✓ ✓
B ~~B~~ ✓
C ~~C~~ ✓
D ~~D D D~~ ✓
E ~~E E E E E E~~ ✓ ✓ ✓ ✓ ✓ ✓
F ✓ ✓
G ~~G G~~ ✓
H ~~H H~~
I ~~I I I I I~~ ✓ ✓ ✓ ✓
J ✓
K ~~K~~
L ~~L L~~ ✓ ✓
M ~~M M~~
N ~~N N N~~ ✓ ✓

O ~~O O O O~~ ✓ ✓ ✓ ✓
P ~~P~~ ✓
Q ~~Q~~
R ~~R R R~~ ✓ ✓
S ~~S~~ ✓ ✓ ✓
T ~~T T~~ ✓ ✓ ✓ ✓
U ~~U U~~ ✓ ✓
V ~~V~~ ✓
W ~~W W~~
X ✓
Y ~~Y~~ ✓
Z ✓
? ~~? ?~~

Tile-Tracking Sheet 3

~~A A A A A A A~~ A A
~~E E E E E E E E~~ E E E
~~I I I I I I~~ I I I
~~O O O O O~~ O O O
~~U U U~~ U

J K ~~Q~~ X ~~Z~~
B B ~~C C~~ ~~D D D~~ D
~~F~~ F ~~G G~~ G ~~H H~~
~~L~~ L L L M M ~~N N N N~~ N N
~~P~~ P
~~R R R R~~ R R
~~S S S~~ S
~~T T T~~ T T
V V W W ~~Y~~ Y
~~Y Y~~

Of course, if you have access to a computer or photocopier, you only need to write or type your tracking sheet out once and then print off a whole batch of them.

Many people still think of tile-tracking as somehow cheating. Coming back to the cards analogy, it has been pointed out that you can't pre-prepare a grid of cards and cross them off as they are played. I certainly wouldn't try it in the local bridge club or poker casino. But in Scrabble, given that you have pen and paper in front of you to keep the score, it would be perverse not to allow it. If I've got seven tiles left on my rack and you've got the last five, there is a far greater level of skill attached to winning the game if each of us knows what the other is holding, rather than both just shooting in the dark.

Note that you shouldn't cross tiles off your tracking sheet when you pick them; you may decide to change, so only eliminate them when they are actually played. If tile-tracking is new to you, you may find you forget to track the occasional move – usually after a bonus – but with the majority crossed off, you can usually rescue the situation with a quick count. If both the **B**s have been played and you discover you have only crossed off one, chances are that it's one of the moves in which a **B** was played that you forgot about.

Predicting what your opponent will do

So, you know what your opponent has on his final rack. (To avoid a lot of tiresome uses of 'he or she' and 'his or her', let's say in this instance that the opponent is male.) Try to work out what his highest move is, especially if he has a high-scoring tile. If his next-highest move is substantially less, play something to block the high-scoring move – unless by doing so you deny yourself a sufficiently high score for your own highest move. Do the arithmetic. If I score 16 here, he gets 32 there. But if I block his 32, even though it only scores me 12 (so I'm 'down four'), he can only get 20, so he's 'down 12'. So it must be worth it to block his 32 point move.

Playing out

The other main consideration in endgame play is playing out (i.e. getting rid of all your tiles to finish the game) as quickly as possible. When you're down to your final tiles, try to play a move which will allow you to play all your remaining tiles in the next move. That means you need two places to play out, so that even if your opponent blocks one, you still have the other. Conversely, you must look to see if your opponent only has one place to play out – and if so, block it.

It's surprising how often it's worth accepting a score that might be lower than your optimal score by quite a few points, if it enables you to play out at your next move. You deny your opponent another score, and get the value of his remaining tiles added to your score, and he gets the same value deducted. That usually adds up to a sizable swing that can make all the difference in a tight game.

Playing an end game

Have a look at the board opposite from my good friend and Scrabble genius Phil Appleby. You are 13 points behind, and, having tile-tracked, you know your opponent has **D E K O R**. What points do you need to consider for your next move? What would you play? Take a few minutes to examine the board and decide what you would do.

Your opponent has one place to play out – by playing **FORKED** using the floating **F** near the bottom left-hand corner. You must block this play, and play something that will enable you to play out in the following move. Look for his next-best score, and work out whether you can score enough to win the game. If not, look again.

Assuming your opponent has a good knowledge of three- and four-letter words, he can play **KEB** or **KOB** on the top left Triple Word square, for 27. **DREK** or **DEEK**, using the **E** of **OYEZ** and also making **KO**, notches up 25. His best score is **ROED**, played directly under the **AINE** of **MORAINE**,

Your rack: **I I N O S S T**

also making **AR**, **IO**, **NE** and **JOBED**, which scores 33.

Endgame problems can get very complex, and computer power (not available during a real game, obviously) has to be harnessed to be sure of getting the optimal path for each player. One good play for you would be **MOIST**, using the **M** of **MORAINE** and making four two-letter words. That scores you 27, and blocks your opponent's **FORKED**. If he now plays his next-best **ROED**, you go down to the bottom-right Triple Word square and play out with **SIN/WARDENS/GI**, which would give you a 14-point win.

If your opponent, rather than playing **ROED**, blocks your **SIN** outplay, such as by playing **GO/OD**, he gets a much smaller score and you can win by playing **SIN** elsewhere, such as making **SIN/JOBES**.

The two important things here are that you blocked his **FORKED**, and you left yourself more than one place to play out your remaining letters. And unlike other Scrabble situations, where the best move is all about the balance of probabilities, maximizing your chances, seeing which way the wind's blowing and hoping for the best, the working out of a winning endgame can, if you can find the right path, give you a guaranteed win without trusting to luck. It's an immensely satisfying feeling to get it right and know you've won a game that, with a little less care, you could have lost.

Scrabble facts – *Tournaments and most clubs use special timers to limit the length of time a game can last. You generally get 25 minutes each to play all your moves – the timer has two clock-faces (or, these days, digital displays), one for each player, and your own side is only ticking while it's your turn. This means you can't hold everyone up by sitting for an hour working out your endgame strategy. If you go to a club where timers are used, they will be fully explained to you before you play, so don't be fazed by them.*

Developing endgame strategy

Endgames need a lot of practice. As you can see in the example above, they also need a good knowledge of the shorter words. And one further difficulty – it's much harder working out what your opponent might do, even if you know what tiles he is holding, when you can't physically see those tiles in front of you.

In a recent game, I worked out that my opponent's final tiles were **D E E E M R T**, and duly blocked what I thought was her best score (probably something like **ME** for 20) while making sure I could play out next move. What I completely missed was that she had the word **METERED**, which she duly played with great glee for around 70 points to win the game. I wouldn't have missed **METERED** if I'd had those tiles in front of me on my own rack (or at least I hope I wouldn't), but it's that much harder when you're looking at the letters scribbled in a corner of a crowded piece of paper.

There are other elements to endgame strategy. For example, if you have a high-scoring tile which you can't score much with on the board as it stands, you might be able to set yourself up an unblockable high score with it next time.

Your rack: **A A C D E I X**

Opponent's rack: **N R U Y**

Without showing the whole board, let's assume there is nowhere for you to score much with your **X**. If you play **ACID** in the second-top row, also making **AA** and **CH**, you can then play out in the next move with **AXE** along the top row, also making **ACH/XI/ED** and scoring 66 points. If your opponent uses the **D** to make **DUN** or **DRY**, you still get 60 for **AX** – not an outplay, but probably enough to win even a semi-close game.

The outcome from preparing an unblockable high score.

It will rarely, if ever, work out quite as neatly as that, but always see if you can use your perfect knowledge of your opponent's rack to set yourself up a move like this if you have a high-scoring tile on your rack at the endgame.

12 Other forms of Scrabble

Over the years, some players have taken to experimenting with other ways of playing Scrabble, apart from sitting facing your opponent across a table and playing to the standard rules of the game. Various ideas have come and gone. Some take hold and become popular alternatives, others vanish almost as soon as they appear.

Junior Scrabble

Many people will have had their first introduction to the game in the form of Junior Scrabble or some other children's version of the game. Junior Scrabble has a board with preprinted words in a Scrabble game format, and players have to pick tiles which match the letters on the board and play them in the appropriate squares. The back of the board has yet another version of the game, somewhat more challenging than Junior Scrabble but not quite up to the complexity of the real thing.

Simpsons Scrabble

Mattel currently produce a range of Scrabble games for younger players, including Simpsons Scrabble, which involves among other things Bart stealing Triple Word squares from an ever more exasperated Homer. This author has not had the pleasure of playing Simpsons Scrabble yet, but it sounds immense fun.

Computer Scrabble

No game would be complete today without its computer version. There are various forms of Computer Scrabble for sale, most of which have features such as allowing you to play the computer at different levels, thus putting your opponent at a standard of anything from beginner to expert. You can set the computer to tell you what it would have played with your letters, and, being a computer, it has the annoying property, when set at the top level, of never missing a seven-letter word or other good play, thus gradually shredding your confidence as it points out all the bonuses you missed. Happily you can always switch it off, an option I would dearly love to have with certain human opponents I can think of.

Duplicate Scrabble

Another way of playing the game is Duplicate Scrabble. This is a method used for large tournaments, and involves all the players sitting at their own individual table with their own set. You do not have an opponent – or rather, everyone else in the room is your opponent. A Master of Ceremonies will draw seven tiles, and all players then have a set time to come up with the highest-scoring move they can make with those tiles. Each player scores according to his or her move, but then the highest-scoring move is announced, and all the players who did not play that move remove their own play from their board, and substitute the highest-scoring move.

Play continues with the MC drawing as many tiles as are necessary to replenish the rack to seven in the normal way, and all the players, using the tiles which are already on the board and their new rack of seven tiles, again have to find the highest-scoring move they can. This process goes on until all the tiles have been used or no further plays are possible, with the player achieving the highest total for the game being the winner.

Pros and cons of Duplicate Scrabble

The advantage of Duplicate is that the luck element is eliminated; every player has the exact same rack and the exact same board at every move; thus, in theory, the best player should always win. While this is a big advantage, there are a number of downsides to Duplicate. The skills of rack management, such as accepting a lower score this time in the hope of a much higher one next time, do not apply. You are simply looking for the highest score you can every time; if you can get one extra point for adding an **S**, you do so. There is no question of playing in certain positions to try to open up the board or close it off. Only the score for that move is important.

Duplicate Scrabble also loses an important social aspect of the game. There is less to talk about afterwards. The 'If-only-I'd-played-this-you-wouldn't-have-been-able-to-play-that' type of conversation so beloved of Scrabble players doesn't take place. No clever play such as holding back a **U** because there are only half a dozen tiles left in the bag and the **Q** has not yet been played. If you need that **U** to obtain the highest possible score now, you have to play it.

Duplicate is the form of the game used for tournaments in France. It has been tried a few times in the UK but has never proved popular, and you will be most unlikely to come across it unless you cross the Channel (where they will sneakily place you at the additional disadvantage of having to play in French).

If Only

A few other unofficial variations of Scrabble have emerged. If Only allows you to turn one of your tiles over each shot and use it as a blank, as long as you score at least 50. You can then replace that 'blank' later with the letter it represents, and reuse the original tile. For instance, you play **SQUEEZE** with the **Z** represented by a tile turned over to look like a blank. You, but not your opponent, know that the tile is really a **K**. Later in the game, your rack reads **J H U C Z L E**. You place the **Z**, right way up, in **SQUEEZE**, lifting the **K**. Then you turn your **J** over to look like a blank, call it a **C**, and hey presto – the semantic mishmash of **J H U C Z L E** becomes **CHUCKLE**.

If Only is a fast, open form of the game with bonuses aplenty and very high scores. It's useful for honing your bonus-finding skills, and as players generally enjoy this aspect of the game more than the board-blocking negative side, If Only friendlies are often played at tournaments at the end of the day as a wind-down from the rigours of the official games.

Super Scrabble

Some time ago, an Australian player came up with **Super Scrabble**. He cut a number of Scrabble boards into sections and created a larger board, something like 25 x 25 as against the standard 15 x 15. He added Quadruple and even Quintuple Letter and Word squares, and played with two or perhaps three full sets of tiles. I believe there was even a 'wrap-around' option, where, if you came to the end of the row or bottom of the column, you could continue your word by going back to the beginning of the row or top of the column, if the space was free. A version of Super Scrabble is available but not in most shops. It's best to master the standard game before you worry about going Super.

Scrabble Poker

Finally, I can add my own modest creation to the panoply of Scrabble-related games with Scrabble Poker, a combination of Scrabble and my other favourite game, though one at which I remain distressingly and impoverishingly inept, poker. Each player picks, or is dealt, two tiles face down and one face up. There is then a round of betting in normal poker fashion, with each player calling, raising or folding as he or she sees fit. Another four tiles are dealt to each player, face up, with a further round of betting at the conclusion of each round of dealing.

When each player has seven tiles, five open and the other two known only to the holder, there is a final round of betting. The winner is the player who can make the longest word from his or her seven tiles (unlike real poker, you can use all seven to make your hand, not just your best five). In the event of two or more players making words of equal length, the winner is the one whose word has the highest face value.

It may never take the casinos or the on-line poker sites by storm, but I and a few of my friends like it as an occasional alternative to the Full Scrabble Monty, as it were. The civilizing influence of Scrabble tends to ensure stakes stay as pennies rather than pounds, and it's another good exercise in bonus-spotting, as well as giving practice in five- and six-letter words, which can sometimes get rather swept aside in the real game in the rush to master twos, threes, and fours, and to learn large numbers of ever more unlikely sevens.

None of these alternatives will ever usurp the genuine article from its position of supremacy, remaining rather the boisterous offspring of a serene and untroubled mother. Difficult enough to be challenging, yet not so arcane as to be open only to a select few, sociable, with the right combination of luck and skill, it can be tinkered with, but not improved upon. It is a tribute to the original game that it can admit so many other versions yet still remain effortlessly superior to all of them.

13 Taking it further

So, you've had your appetite whetted for trying to move your Scrabble game up a level or two. You want to squeeze more points out of every move with neat little parallel plays using two- and three-letter words, you want to play some impressive bonuses, and then eke out a win with a well-thought-out endgame. The only problem is, if your Scrabble-playing friends and relatives don't want to come on this journey with you, you are pitched into an endless round of 'What does that mean?' and 'That's not a proper word'.

Even showing Auntie Mary that **XU**, **JIZ** or **ETESIAN** is there in black and white in the *Collins Scrabble Lists* is unlikely to appease her. Learning useful words and good techniques to improve your game is seen as unsportsmanlike, almost cheating. So your next move has to be to take a deep breath and move into the wonderful world of your local Scrabble club.

Clubs and tournaments

People can have some odd ideas about Scrabble clubs – that's if they realize they exist at all. They are assumed to be patronized solely by either elderly ladies in pink cardigans or geeky guys taking an evening off from working out the square root of minus one. While I can't quite guarantee you won't meet anyone at all like that, most Scrabble club members are normal, well-adjusted people who want nothing more than a sociable evening out and a good game of Scrabble.

> *Scrabble facts* – *There are about 330 Scrabble clubs in Britain, and a further 200 or so in schools.*

You can find the whereabouts of your local Scrabble club by writing to:

Scrabble Clubs UK

Mattel House

Vanwall Business Park

Vanwall Road

Maidenhead

Berkshire

SL6 4UB.

Or if you're of a more technological turn of mind, try putting 'Scrabble' and your home town into your internet search engine and see what comes up.

What happens at a Scrabble Club?

It's impossible to be definitive, as each will be run in a slightly different way. Some will have a very informal approach, where you just turn up and play anyone else who is waiting for a game. Others are more structured, where you all start at the same time and the organizer tells you who to play. Others again have a league table where you have to play everyone, or everyone in your division, once or twice in a season (however long a season may be), but within that you arrange your own games at times to suit.

However, a few things are pretty much universal at any Scrabble club in the country (and, I imagine, the world). There will be a meeting place and a regular evening when the club meets (although the large and venerable London Scrabble League, of which I have had the honour of being chairman, arranges four-player fixtures in members' homes). There will either be tables about the size of card tables for individual games, or longer trestle tables that can accommodate a few games at a time. Players generally supply their own Scrabble sets and other paraphernalia, so take yours if possible. Crucially, tea and coffee will be supplied either as part of your entry fee or subscription, or for a small charge.

There are a few other ways in which playing at a club may be different from how you are used to playing at home.

De luxe sets

Most clubs insist on, or at least give preference to, de luxe sets; these have boards which are on a turntable so that they can be moved to face each player, and tiles that click into the square on which they are played so that they don't move around when the board is turned, accidentally nudged or otherwise moved. Nothing detracts more from the pleasure of the game than continually having to realign the tiles so that you can read the words properly, or having to twist your neck to try to read the board upside-down. You don't read a book or newspaper upside-down, so why try to do it with a Scrabble board?

Smooth tiles

As you now know, the most valuable tiles in the bag are the blanks. For that reason, it is slightly unsatisfactory that you can sometimes, accidentally or deliberately, feel that a tile in the bag is a blank. Smooth tiles prevent any suspicion that a player has been feeling in the bag for a blank tile. The newest sets do contain smooth tiles. However, there are many older sets around which do not contain smooth tiles. Some Clubs insist that you play with smooth tiles.

Playing one opponent at a time

Quite simply, Scrabble is a game for two players. The rules that come with your set may say you can play with up to four, but the two-person game is far superior. You cannot form a strategy, nor can you plan ahead in any way, if there are two or even three more people to play between your last turn and your next one. Apart from that, it's just boring playing with three or four players – you are only involved in the game a third or a quarter of the time, and if one or two of your opponents are slow, you can have an interminable wait till it comes round to you again. Sure, you can be looking for what you might play when it eventually becomes your turn, but only to a limited extent. You have no way of knowing if your opponents' plays will drive a coach and horses through the place you were going to make your move – or if they might give you a better one.

In club and tournament play, if the numbers are odd, one person will sit out for a round. Alternatively, one player may take on two players at once, but in two completely separate games on two separate boards. This is an excellent way of sharpening up your Scrabble reflexes, rather like a chess simul, a form of chess match where one (usually superior) player takes on a number of others simultaneously.

Use of *Collins Scrabble Lists* for all adjudications

It's very annoying when you play a word, only to have it disallowed – especially if, the week before, you were allowed to play it. It's even more maddening if your opponent the week before was allowed to play it. Many clubs use *Collins Scrabble Lists* to adjudicate on any challenges. This lists every allowable word in strict alphabetical order except that very long words, those with 10 letters or more, are confined to a separate section at the end. For more on allowable word forms see the back of this book.

Creating your own list of words

If you are not using *Collins Scrabble Lists*, then the second-best solution is to start your own list. If you allow, say, **NUBILER**, put it on an 'allowed' list and keep it with your set or tuck it into your dictionary. Similarly, if you decide that **EDIBLER** is a comparative too far, it goes on your 'disallowed list'. Then, when the word comes up next week or next year, you can at least be consistent. But you still have the problem of deciding which list it goes on in the first place – and when one of you has played the word and there are only the two of you there, a one-each stalemate on whether the word should be valid is almost inevitable. The best solution is to buy *Collins Scrabble Lists*. If it's in there, the word is valid; if it ain't, it ain't.

Playing to win

As I've emphasized throughout this book, it's not what you score that counts, it's whether you score more than your opponent. It's a statement of the obvious, surely. Don't we always play a game to win?

In the early days of the National Scrabble Championship (NSC), the winner was the person with the highest total score over a set number of games. It didn't matter whether you actually won the games or not. So if you could score 500 points or so in all your games, even if you lost one or two, this was better than plodding along scoring 300–400 but making sure you always won. This led to a highly artificial form of the game where your opponent effectively became your partner where you played a very open game, which means you tried to make lots of places on the board where bonus words would fit in.

Matchplay Scrabble

Eventually most players realized this was a silly way to play, and what was called Matchplay Scrabble took over. Quite simply, this meant playing to win: scoring 500 is pointless if your opponent gets 501. At the end of the tournament, the player who had won the most games was the winner.

Having said that, you can't afford to neglect the possibility of high scores, because players on the same number of wins are ranked according to their 'spread'. This is the total points scored by you minus the total points scored by all your opponents – the equivalent of goal difference in football. So, at least at the beginning of a tournament or club competition, and at the end if you're in contention, it's nice to stick in a really high score, as long as your opponent doesn't score almost as much (or even more). Note that spread is a very different thing from score. Spread takes into account not just your score but also what your opponent scores against you, so you must always be alert to denying chances to your opponent as well as getting a good score yourself.

So what all that boils down to for you is this. Don't just think of your move as a score of a certain number of points. See how it affects the board before you play it. Check if it opens up any high-scoring opportunities, which your opponent is almost bound to take. If it does, try to find an alternative, less risky move elsewhere.

The playing of **CARE** would be a risky move here, as you have opened a triple-word chance for your opponent if he has an **S**, **D**, **R**, **T** or even **X** for **CAREX**.

Both players keep the score

If you are playing to win, it follows that you need to know whether you are winning or losing, and by how much, at any particular time. If you're behind, you may need to take a bit of a risk and make some openings. If you're ahead, you should be trying to close things up. So make sure you keep the score. If your opponent is of a like mind – fine, both of you can then keep the score. In any case, it's useful to have a check – mistakes are easily made.

When you try all these things for yourself at a club, as well as involving yourself in the higher standard of play, you will be rewarded by finding Scrabble suddenly just feels like a better game.

Differences between club and home play

There are a few other ways in which club play and home play differ. The moment when your shot is over is defined carefully. If timers are being used, it's the moment you press the button to stop your own timer and start your opponent's; without timers, it's the moment you announce your score. Until that point of no return is passed, you can take your tiles back and change your mind.

Challenging

From this, it follows that you shouldn't challenge your opponent's move until he has pressed the timer or announced that score; by doing so, you alert him to the fact that you think the word is wrong, and he may take the opportunity to think again.

Lifting the tile-bag

Another thing newcomers to a club find quite odd is the sight of players lifting the bag well clear of the table when they pick new tiles. The rule is that the bag should be lifted to shoulder height, thus precluding any possibility of cheating by having a sly look in the bag as it lies on the table. As with the 'feelable blanks', this is not to say that cheating was rife before this rule was introduced; merely that it is better to eliminate the possibility of cheating rather than having any unwarranted suspicions lingering around the name of an honest player.

No late changes

Apart from a few details introduced mainly to facilitate the use of timers, the actual rules of the game at a club are exactly the same as you are used to at home – with one exception: you can't change when there are fewer than seven tiles left in the bag.

This rule was introduced back in the dark days when a **Q** picked late in the game was likely to be unplayable. It prevented a player throwing a **Q** back into the bag at the last moment, in an attempt to foist it on his opponent. Nowadays, with **QI**, **QAT** and so on at our disposal, a last-minute **Q** is not such a nightmare, but the rule persists. It may be fair to say that you shouldn't be allowed to put a **Q**, a **J**, a **V**, or some other unplayable letter back in the bag at the very end, forcing your opponent to pick it if he wants to make a move. On the other hand, a more hard-nosed player may think it should all be part of the game. At the moment, once there are six tiles in the bag or fewer, whatever you've got on your rack is what you're stuck with.

Tournament play

This has the same rules as club play, but it's a difference of atmosphere more than anything else. Everyone is trying that bit harder and their play is that bit sharper.

Tournaments are generally divided into divisions, so that you play people roughly of your own standard. Also, tournaments are usually played under the Swiss system, which means that, as far as possible, you play someone on the same number of wins as yourself. However they are arranged, everyone plays in every round, so there is no danger of travelling half the length of the country and only playing one game because you lose in the first round.

A one-day tournament will normally be held over six rounds. Weekend tournaments over two days can have between 11 and 16 rounds. Sometimes, usually on a holiday weekend, they are played over three days, with between 17 and 19 rounds. Occasionally there are even weeklong tournaments. If you fancy having a go at a tournament, get in touch with the Association of British Scrabble Players. The ABSP regulates tournament play in the UK, and you'll find a very useful calendar of events on their website, **www.absp.org.uk**

Reaching for the top

One of the best aspects of getting involved in the Scrabble club and tournament scene is that, even if you don't immediately feel ready to take on the very best players, you can still mix with them, get to know them, and learn from them. With most competitions being divided into divisions, you can rub shoulders with the top players without the risk to your ego of actually having to play them. Go along to some tournaments, especially the bigger ones and you will find that restaurant, bar, and tea-room are a mix of potential world champions, the greenest of newcomers, and everything in between.

Once you've taken that first step of venturing along to a local club, the whole vista of how to get more out of Scrabble starts to open out for you. You will find out where to get hold of the better equipment that adds so much to the game but may not be available in your local shops. Many players now have personalized boards made to their own design (so much classier than a personalized number plate). Round boards, which can be turned without knocking over racks, cups of tea, etc., are particularly popular. Someone will tell you about computer programs, electronic pocket gizmos of various kinds, or even good old-fashioned books, any or all of which you can use to improve your word power and check where you might have done better in an actual game.

At this stage in developing your Scrabble skills, don't worry about tournaments but just concentrate on getting a good grip of some of the basics in this book, such as the twos, the threes, making good use of **JQXZ**, trying for bonuses by balancing your rack between vowels and consonants, keeping those bonus-friendly tiles (especially blank and **S**) and learning some of the sevens and eights that they make. Then either get your regular opponents to do the same, or join a Scrabble club. I wish you many hours of happy and stimulating Scrabble playing.

Allowable word forms

If you haven't, or haven't yet, got *Collins Scrabble Lists*, you and your
fellow-players will have to do a bit of adjudicating from time to time.
A dictionary will generally list only a base word, such as **TABLE**. It will not
specifically show **TABLES**, **TABLED**, **TABLING** or **TABLINGS**. Before starting
play it's worth agreeing a few guidelines as to what you're going to allow
and what you aren't.

Plurals

Nouns, fairly obviously, have a plural. But all nouns? If you watch
Countdown you will have become familiar with the concept of 'count
nouns' and 'mass nouns'. A count noun is something you can have more
than one of, and therefore the noun takes a plural. **MAN**, **HORSE** and
BANANA are all count nouns with obvious plurals. It needn't be a thing
you can touch – **DAY**, **LIE** and **FEELING** are also count nouns.

The problems start, if you allow them to, with the mass noun.
Can you pluralize words like **TENNIS**, **CALCITE** and **FLU**? *Countdown* will
often say 'no', declaring that they are mass nouns, so you can't have more
than one of them. My advice about this is – forget it. Any noun can have a
plural. Go ahead and allow **TENNISES**, **CALCITES** and **FLUS**. *Collins
Scrabble Lists* certainly does.

What is not always so easy to work out is what the plural actually is.
We know that it is usually formed by adding –s. There are some well-known
exceptions – so well-known, in fact, that you barely register them. Nouns
ending in –s, –ch or –sh all add –es, for example **TENNISES**, **CHURCHES**
and **BRUSHES**. (As usual, there are exceptions to the exceptions – words

ending in the Scottish **ch**, like **LOCH**, just add **–s** in the plural).

Words ending in **–y** preceded by a consonant change the **–y** to **–ies**, so we have **FLIES, BERRIES**, etc. And of course we have **MEN, MICE, SHEEP** and plenty of other common irregular plurals.

But what is the plural of **TROUT**? Usually it would just be **TROUT**, as in 'I caught six trout.' But could it ever be valid to say **TROUTS**? Remember **TROUT** has an informal meaning of a silly or unpleasant person. 'The neighbours round here are a right bunch of trout'. That sounds odd. 'A right bunch of trouts', surely. And sometimes you need a bit more technical knowledge. Is **RADIUSES** an acceptable alternative to **RADII** as the plural of **RADIUS**? It's at moments like these that you do need to go to the dictionary – preferably always the same one. For the record, *Collins Scrabble Lists* allows **TROUTS** and **RADIUSES**.

Verbs

What about verbs? Again, it's fairly simple on the face of it. We have the **–s**, **–ed** and **–ing** endings; thus **CONTAIN** leads to **CONTAINS, CONTAINED** and **CONTAINING**. If the verb ends in **–e**, drop the **e** before adding **–ed** or **–ing**, as in **STROKED, STROKING**. And we have a similar **–y** adjustment to the one we have with nouns, as in **MARRIES, MARRIED**. Then there is the doubling, in certain circumstances, of a final consonant before **–ed** and **–ing**, as in **STRUMMED, STRUMMING**. That's quite a few exceptions already, all of which we handle in normal speech and writing without a moment's thought. But if we think of short, simple verbs, there seem to be more exceptions than adherents to the rule – **RUN, SWIM, BUILD, TAKE, GO, DO, SPEAK, PAY, EAT, DRINK** and **MAKE** all deviate from the **–ed** form. Again, there is no substitute for a good dictionary if you want to be sure of the irregularities.

Adjectives

Now for the adjectives. Before the advent of *Collins Scrabble Lists*, no element of word adjudication caused more problems than whether you could add **–er** and **–est** to an adjective. **POLITER, STERILEST, WHOLER, HONESTEST, UNFITTER, LIVEST, DEADEST** – these and many like them caused hours of harmless merriment, and the occasional tantrum, as their acceptability or otherwise was debated. There is no doubt now which ones are not allowed (**STERILEST** and **WHOLER**).

Glossary of terms

Only terms used in this book are included.

ABSP   The Association of British Scrabble Players, the official organization which regulates tournament play and carries out other associated functions.

affix   A prefix or suffix.

anagram   A word which comprises the same letters as another word, but in a different order.

big tiles   The high-scoring tiles – **J**, **Q**, **X** and **Z**. In some contexts also includes the **S**s and blanks.

blank   One of two tiles in the set which the holder may use to represent any letter.

block   To play a move which prevents an opponent from playing in that part of the board.

blocked board *or* **game**   A board with few positions where moves are possible. Opposite of open board or game.

blocker   A move which prevents an opponent from playing, either a specific move or in a particular part of the board; a word which cannot be extended either at the front or the back.

bonus   The extra 50 points awarded for playing all seven tiles in one move; or a move which achieves this.

break up   To play some of a promising combination of letters.

challenge   To query the validity of a word played by an opponent. The word must then be checked in a dictionary or *Collins Scrabble Lists*.

change   To use one's turn by putting unwanted tiles back into the bag and picking new ones, rather than by placing a move on the board.

combination   Any stated group of letters.

common letter   A low-scoring letter of which there are several in the set; or a letter which is part of a word on the board both horizontally and vertically.

compound word   A word made out of two smaller words, which combines the meanings of both of them.

consonant-heavy   Describes a rack with too many consonants.

contraction   A word formed from a longer word, but with some of the letters omitted, although the meaning is unchanged.

count noun   A noun representing something of which there can be one or more than one, e.g. table. *Opposite* of mass noun.

Criss-Crosswords   The name of an early version of Scrabble.

crosswise play   The playing of a move which creates only one new word on the board. *Opposite* of parallel play.

discard (tiles)   To replace unwanted tiles in the bag, in order to draw new ones.

distribution   The frequency with which each letter appears in a standard set of tiles.

Double Letter square (score)   A square, on most boards coloured light blue, which doubles the point value of any tile played on it.

Double Word square (score)   A square, on most boards coloured pink, which doubles the point value of any word which has one of its letters on it.

draw (tiles)   To pick tiles from the bag.

duplicate   The same letter appearing two or more times on the same rack.

endgame   The final stages of a game, when knowledge of the letters which are or may be on an opponent's rack affects the moves a player makes.

end hook   A letter which can be placed at the end of a word to make another word.

face value   The number of points scored by any tile, word or move, unaffected by Premium squares.

floater   A tile on the board, in such a position that it can be used as part of another word.

frequency   The number of times a given letter appears in a standard set.

front hook   A letter which can be placed at the beginning of a word to make another word.

hook   A letter which can be placed at the beginning or end of a word to make another word; to play a move which uses a letter in this way.

interlocking   Joining tiles to those already on the board to make new words; all moves in a game except the opening move must be interlocking.

It   The name of an early version of Scrabble.

leave (the)   The tiles left on a player's rack, after playing a move but before picking fresh tiles from the bag.

Lexiko   The name of the original version of Scrabble.

mass noun   A noun representing something which cannot be counted, e.g. fairness. *Opposite* of count noun.

Matchplay   Playing solely to win the game, without relevance to the score achieved.

one-pointer   A tile worth one point, i.e. the commonest letters most useful for making bonus words – **A E I L N O R S T U**.

open board *or* **game**   A board with several positions where moves, especially high-scoring moves, are possible. *Opposite of* blocked board or game.

outplay   A move which enables a player to play all his or her remaining tiles, there being no more tiles left in the bag – therefore, the last move of the game.

parallel play A move in which a word is placed parallel to another word or words on the board, thus also forming one or more vertical words if the main word is played horizontally, and vice versa. *Opposite of* crosswise play.

play out To play all one's remaining tiles, there being no more tiles left in the bag, thus playing the last move of the game.

point value The number of points scored by a given tile.

prefix A combination of letters which can often be found at the beginning of a word.

Premium square A square on the board which awards more than face value to a letter or word played on it – a Double Letter, Double Word, Triple Letter, or Triple Word score.

rack The wooden or plastic stand on which a player places his or her tiles; the letters held by a player at any particular time.

rack management The playing of tiles in such a way as to increase one's chances of having a bonus word, or other high-scoring move, on the next or subsequent turn.

'six plus one' list A list of seven-letter words which can be formed by the addition of one other letter to a particular combination of six letters. Similarly 'six plus two' list or 'seven plus one' list.

spread In a game or tournament, the total number of points scored by a player, minus the total points scored against him or her. A spread may therefore be positive or negative.

suffix A combination of letters which can often be found at the end of a word.

Swiss system A method of organizing fixtures at large tournaments, where each player is, as far as possible, matched against another on the same number of wins.

synergy The property of certain combinations of letters of combining well with each other to form words.

take A word is said to take a particular letter when that letter can be added to the word to form another word. A word may take a letter at the front or at the end.

tile Any of the one hundred pieces, each (except the two blanks) representing a letter, which are used to play the game by forming words on the board.

tile-tracking Noting which tiles have been played, and modifying one's play accordingly to take account of which tiles are likely to be picked or which tiles the opponent is, or may be, holding.

Triple Letter square (score) A square, on most boards coloured dark blue, which triples the point value of any letter played on it.

Triple Word square (score) A square, on most boards coloured red, which triples the point value of any word which has one of its letters on it.

vowel–consonant balance *or* **vowel–consonant split** The number of vowels and consonants on the rack, or remaining in the bag, at any particular time.

vowel-heavy Describes a rack with too many vowels.

Z-three A three-letter word containing a **Z**.

Quick reference lists

*Alphabetical list of **all** two-letter words*

AA	AB	AD	AE	AG	AH	AI	AL	AM	AN
	AR	AS	AT	AW	AX	AY			
BA	BE	BI	BO	BY					
CH									
DA	DE	DI	DO						
EA	ED	EE	EF	EH	EL	EM	EN	ER	ES
	ET	EX							
FA	FE	FY							
GI	GO	GU							
HA	HE	HI	HM	HO					
ID	IF	IN	IO	IS	IT				
JA	JO								
KA	KI	KO	KY						
LA	LI	LO							
MA	ME	MI	MM	MO	MU	MY			
NA	NE	NO	NU	NY					
OB	OD	OE	OF	OH	OI	OM	ON	OO	OP
	OR	OS	OU	OW	OX	OY			
PA	PE	PI	PO						
QI									
RE									
SH	SI	SO	ST						
TA	TE	TI	TO						
UG	UH	UM	UN	UP	UR	US	UT		
WE	WO								
XI	XU								
YA	YE	YO	YU						
ZA	ZO								

Alphabetical list of useful three-letter words appearing in this book

AAH	AAL	AAS	ACH	ADZ	AIA	AUA	AUE	AYU
BAA	BEZ	BIZ						
CAA	CAZ	CHA	CHE	CHI	COZ	CUZ		
DEX	DZO							
EAU	ECH							
FAA	FEZ	FIZ						
GJU	GOX							
HMM	HOX							
ICH								
JAP	JEE	JIZ	JOE					
KEX	KYE	KYU						
MAA	MIZ	MOZ						
OCH	OHM							
QAT	QIS	QUA						
RAJ	RAX	REX						
SAZ	SEZ	SKY	SUQ					
TAJ								
UVA								
VAU	VAV	VOX						
WEX	WOX							
XIS								
ZAG	ZAX	ZEP	ZIG	ZOA	ZOS			

Alphabetical list of useful words using J, Q, X and Z

AFLAJ	AQUA	AX	AXE	
EX				
FALAJ	FAQIR			
IXIA				
JA	JO	JORAM	JORUM	JUGA
OX				
PREX				
QADI	QAID	QANAT	QAT	QI
	QIBLA	QOPH	QUATE	QUINE
SOREX				
TALAQ	TRANQ			
WAQF				
XENIA				
XI	XU			
ZA	ZAIRE	ZEIN	ZILA	ZO

Answers to puzzles

CHALLENGE NO. 1

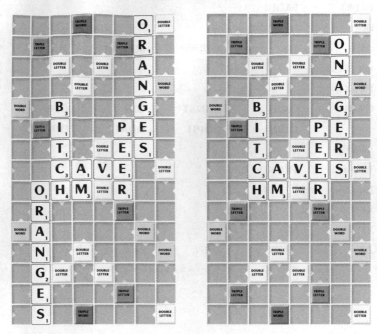

Your rack is **A E G N O R S**

Finding **ORANGES** should not have presented you with too much of a problem. But the importance of the two- and three-letter words is shown by the fact that you can't fit **ORANGES** in without either remembering **PE** and **ES**, or noticing that unlikely hook of turning **HM** into **OHM**.

Incidentally, both those moves put a letter in an outer row of the board, and thus open up a possible nine-timer – a word stretching from one Triple Word square to the next, thus having its score multiplied by nine as well as scoring the extra 50, probably scoring about 150 for one move.

This is undesirable, because your opponent gets first crack at it, and if your opponent has also been nursing his or her rack towards a bonus, they might just be ready to step in. That shouldn't stop you from playing **ORANGES** if it's the only bonus you can see, but you'd be better, if you know it, to play **ONAGERS**, in the same column as **ORANGES/PE/ES** but one square down, also making **PE**, **ER** and **CAVES**. That not only scores more but also, and more importantly, doesn't open the nine-timer.

An **onager** is a type of wild ass, but what you should try to remember is the fact that it's an anagram of **ORANGES**, so that next time you find **ORANGES** on your rack, you will have a bigger choice of moves to play.

CHALLENGE NO. 2

Your rack is **DEIJNOS**

Notice how the short word comfortably outscores the longer one, and, in this case, also prevents your opponent from getting much profit out of the Triple Word squares in the top row.

CHALLENGE NO. 3

Your rack is **A E L M Q S U**

Playing **QUALM** opens a bonus spot along the bottom row, and it may be better to forego 10 points by restricting your play to **QUA**. If your opponent's last move was just playing an **N** after **PI** to make **PIN** for six points, it looks like he or she is close to a bonus so **QUA** might be more sensible. Indeed, taking out one of the high-scoring bonus spots by playing **QUALMS** or **SQUEAL** might be more sensible still. If, on the other hand, your opponent has just played **ZO/HO** for 27, he or she probably played for the points and is less likely to have a bonus rack now. Your move will depend on how defensive you want to be, how good you think your opponent is and what sort of a feeling you've got about the whole position.

CHALLENGE NO. 4

1 **ALLURES, LAURELS**

2 **ALLURES** goes in the second column from the right, also making **AR**, **NE** and **NEEDLESS**. **LAURELS** goes in the second row from the bottom, also making **AL**, **TA** and **HILLOCKS**.

Playing **ALLURES**

Playing **LAURELS**

3 **SQUALLER** goes round the **Q**, also making **ST** and **UN**.

Playing **SQUALLER**

CHALLENGE NO. 5

The blank is pretty clearly going to have to be a vowel, and **E** is the most likely, especially with the duplicate **R**. Note that, even if your opponent played **QUINE** and you didn't know it, you do know **EQUINE**, and you're every bit as entitled to play it as old smarty-pants on the other side of the table.

Your rack: **B D O R R S ?**

CHAPTER 7
A BONUS WORD CHALLENGE

Twenty teasers

The unexpected 'hooks' are shown in brackets.

ASPIRIN (ASPIRING)

NIGHTJAR

ENCHANT (PENCHANT)

PASTRAMI

PARQUET OVERTHIN (OVERTHINK)

AWFULLY (LAWFULLY)

LAVISHES (LAVISHEST)

FLAMING (FLAMINGO)

EXPLOITS

ATISHOO

WORDPLAY (SWORDPLAY)

CHATEAU

HEREUPON (THEREUPON/WHEREUPON)

GAZELLE

MULTIPLE (MULTIPLEX)

DIPLOMA

REHEATED (PREHEATED)

RAVIOLI

REFREEZE

CHAPTER 8
A FEW TEASERS

1 You can check the answers. in the appropriate list (**A E I N R S**, etc).

2 **SEEABLE, STAIDLY, RATLIKE, UNQUIET, SUBDEAN, REKEYED, PRONAOS, ELOGIST**

3 **ANGERED** (+ anagrams), **ELATION/TOENAIL, ORGANIC, EMAILED/ LIMEADE, CIGARET, ANEROID, AMNIOTE, LINOCUT**

CHAPTER 9
SOME GREAT PUZZLES TO TRY

1   Through the floating **G: ASTRINGE, REASTING, STEARING, TASERING**
Through the **N: TRANNIES**
Through the **T: INTREATS, NITRATES, STRAITEN, TARTINES, TERTIANS**
Through the **O: ANOESTRI, ARSONITE, NOTARIES, NOTARISE, ROSINATE, SENORITA**
Through the **R: STRAINER**

2   Through the **K: SNEAKIER**
Through the **U: UNEASIER**
Through the **P: NAPERIES**
Through the **N: ANSERINE** (making **MANA** or **MANI**)
Through the **D: ARSENIDE, DENARIES, DRAISENE, NEARSIDE**

3   Through the **E: UNELATED**
Through the **I: UNTAILED**
Through the **U: UNDULATE**

4   Through the **B: BACTERIN**
Through the **U: ANURETIC**
Through the **V: NAVICERT**
Through the **A: CARINATE, CRANIATE**
Through the **C: ACENTRIC**

Useful links

SCRABBLE is a registered trademark owned by Hasbro (US and Canada) and Mattel (rest of the world).

For more information on Scrabble products, visit:
www.scrabble.com
Association of British Scrabble Players:
www.absp.org.uk
National Scrabble Association (of North America):
www2.scrabble-assoc.com
Singapore Scrabble Association:
www.toucanet.com
Netherlands English Scrabble Club:
www.nesc.nl
South African National Scrabble Player's Association (SANSPA):
www.geocities.com/sanspa/home.html
Australian Scrabble Players Association:
www.scrabble.org.au
New Zealand Association of Scrabble Players:
www.scrabble.co.nz
Malta Scrabble Club:
www.scrabblemalta.com
Nigeria Scrabble Federation:
www.nigerianscrabble.com
Collins Official Scrabble Checker:
www.collinslanguage.com/extras/scrabble.aspx

Scrabble Dictionaries
Play to win!

Within the Scrabble range you'll find the perfect companion for all Scrabble games. Settle all those Scrabble squabbles once and for all with the ultimate authority – the Official Scrabble Dictionary range.

For the Tournament Scrabble Player

OFFICIAL SCRABBLE DICTIONARY
(Second edition) £25.00

SCRABBLE LISTS
£10

SCRABBLE WORDS
£10

For those who play for fun

SCRABBLE DICTIONARY:
FRIENDS AND FAMILY EDITION
£12.99

POCKET SCRABBLE DICTIONARY
(Second edition) £9.99

COLLINS GEM
SCRABBLE DICTIONARY £4.99

Find the perfect companion for all levels of Scrabble games

To place an order for any Collins Scrabble titles call our sales team on 0870 787 1732

Collins www.collinslanguage.com

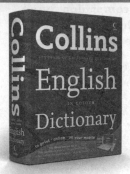
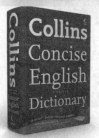
    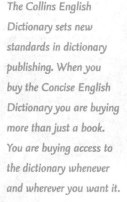